KU-696-050

Contents

Contents

Standard Loan

The College, Merthyr Tydfil - Learning Zone
Tel: 01685 726212 / 726193

© David Mills Daniel 2006

The author and publisher acknowledge material reproduced from
Basic Writings of Saint Thomas Aquinas, Volume I, ed. A. C. Pegis,
Indianapolis/Cambridge: Hackett Publishing Company, 1997,
ISBN 0872203808. Reprinted by permission of Hackett Publishing
Company, Inc. All rights reserved.

British Library Cataloguing in Publication data

A catalogue record for this book is available
from the British Library

0 334 04090 6/978 0 334 04090 3

First published in 2006 by SCM Press
9–17 St Alban's Place,
London N1 0NX

www.scm-canterburypress.co.uk

SCM Press is a division of
SCM-Canterbury Press Ltd

Printed and bound in Great Britain by
Bookmarque Ltd, Croydon, Surrey

Contents

Introduction

The SCM *Briefly* series is designed to enable students and general readers to acquire knowledge and understanding of key texts in philosophy, philosophy of religion, theology and ethics. While the series will be especially helpful to those following university and A-level courses in philosophy, ethics and religious studies, it will in fact be of interest to anyone looking for a short guide to the ideas of a particular philosopher or theologian.

Each book in the series takes a piece of work by one philosopher and provides a summary of the original text, which adheres closely to it, and contains direct quotations from it, thus enabling the reader to follow each development in the philosopher's argument(s). Throughout the summary, there are page references to the original philosophical writing, so that the reader has ready access to the primary text. In the Introduction to each book, you will find details of the edition of the philosophical work referred to.

In *Briefly: Aquinas' Summa Theologica (God, Part II)*, we refer to *Basic Writings of Saint Thomas Aquinas*, vol. I, edited by Anton C. Pegis, 1997, Indianapolis: Hackett Publishing Company, ISBN 0872203808.

Each *Briefly* begins with an Introduction, followed by a chapter on the Context in which the work was written. Who was this writer? Why was this book written? With Some

Introduction

Issues to Consider, and some Suggestions for Further Reading, this *Briefly* aims to get anyone started in their philosophical investigation. The Detailed Summary of the philosophical work is followed by a concise chapter-by-chapter Overview and an extensive Glossary of terms.

Bold type is used in the Detailed Summary and Overview sections to indicate the first occurrence of words and phrases that appear in the Glossary. The Glossary also contains terms used elsewhere in this *Briefly* guide and other terms that readers may encounter in their study of Aquinas' *Summa Theologica*.

Context

Who was Thomas Aquinas?

Thomas Aquinas, the son of Landulf, Count of Aquino, was born at the castle of Roccasecca, near Naples, in 1224 or 1225, and educated at the Benedictine Abbey of Monte Cassino and the University of Naples. While a student, he decided to enter the order of Dominican Friars. This was against the wishes of his parents, who wanted him to become a Benedictine monk. Despite being kidnapped and held prisoner by his family, Aquinas refused to change his mind and, after his release, the Dominicans sent him to the University of Paris in 1245. There he became a student of Albert the Great, the Dominican philosopher and theologian, going with him to the University of Cologne in 1248. Aquinas returned to Paris in 1252, eventually becoming Dominican professor of theology there. He moved to Rome in 1259, where, because of his growing reputation as philosopher, theologian and reconciler of Aristotelian philosophy with Christian teaching, he became adviser to a succession of popes, while continuing to teach (in Rome, Bologna, Paris and Naples) and to write prolifically. In 1274, when he was travelling from Naples to take part in the Second Council of Lyons, he died at the monastery of Fossanuova, near Rome. He was canonized in 1323, and, in 1879, Pope Leo XIII declared that his setting forth of Roman

Catholic teaching was definitive. His books include *De Ente et Essentia* (1254–6), the *Summa Contra Gentiles* (1258–64), the *De Veritate* (1256–9) and the *Summa Theologica* (*Summa Theologiae*, 1265–72).

What is the *Summa Theologica*?

In the introduction to his edition of the *Summa Theologica*, A. C. Pegis describes it as a 'truly monumental synthesis and exposition of Christian thought'; and even after more than eight hundred years, it remains an essential resource for any student of the philosophy of religion or Christian theology. However, the *Summa Theologica* is 'monumental' in length (the first volume of the Pegis edition is almost 1,000 pages), as well as in the quality of its content, so it needs more than one *Briefly* to cover it. The previous *Briefly* (God, Part I) dealt with Aquinas' arguments for the existence of God (the five ways), and his discussion of such issues as the nature and role of sacred doctrine, how we can know and speak about God, and some of God's attributes, such as his goodness, power, simplicity and eternity. This *Briefly* (God, Part II) includes God's unity, knowledge, will, love, justice, mercy and providence, and the issue of predestination. Readers will find it helpful to read the Context of the previous volume, particularly pages 2–7 (the sections about the nature and role of sacred doctrine and God's existence), which deal with the question of what human beings can learn about God by using their reason. Philosophical and theological terms used in this Context are explained in the Glossary.

Future *Brieflys*, also based on Pegis' edition of the *Summa Theologica*, will cover the Divine Persons and Man.

The Existence of God in Things and God's Unity (Questions VIII and XI)

Aquinas considers the claim that God is in and above all things, and also contains them. As he is an all-powerful agent, he does not need to be in all things to affect them, and how can he be in evil things, such as demons?

Aquinas explains that this is largely a problem of the way we refer to God. As the all-powerful creator of everything, nothing actually is remote from God. Just as the soul contains the body, God is in things and contains them, but we say that they are in God, in that they are contained by him. However, things can be said to be remote from him, in that they are unlike him in nature or grace. Even a demon's nature comes from God but, as it has been deformed by sin, God can only be said to be in it to the extent that it is a being.

What about the fact that some people believe that there are many gods? They are simply wrong. There can be only one God who, as his being does not depend on anything else, is supremely being. This one God comprehends in himself the whole perfection of being, and maintains the order of all the diverse things that exist in the universe.

God's Knowledge (Question XIV)

God's knowledge raises important issues. If God is omniscient, he foreknows everything that is going to happen, so how can human beings be free? Aquinas argues that to speak of God's knowledge causing things is like saying that a craftsman's knowledge causes the things he makes. The idea of what he is going to make is in the craftsman's mind and, when he starts work, he makes his artefact in accordance with his plan. However, it requires an act of will before the manufacturing process begins. Therefore, God's will must be joined with what is in his mind before anything is caused.

But is this satisfactory? Or does God's omniscience, his knowing everything that is going to happen, make it difficult to believe in human freedom, in that it seems to make everything that happens, including human choices, seem predetermined and inevitable?

Does God, who is infinitely good, know evil things? Aquinas' response is that to know something perfectly is to know everything that can happen to it. As some good things can be corrupted by evil, God would not know good things perfectly, if he did not know evil things. Indeed, as Aquinas believed that evil is a privation, or lack, of goodness in things (so things are evil to the extent that they lack goodness), God, by knowing good things, must also know evil things.

This kind of account of evil, as lack of good, is a metaphysical or theological one. It does not mean that evil, as it is found in the world, is something negative and insubstantial, which can be ignored or easily endured. Human experience of evil, whether natural (for example, disease or natural disasters) or moral (for example, human violence and greed) is of a positive and destructive force. However, thinking of evil as privation of good helps us to understand that it involves distance from God.

Truth (Question XVI)

Time and again in the *Summa Theologica*, Aquinas shows that many of the problems human beings have in thinking and talking about God, an infinite being, arise from the limitations and ambiguities of human language. It is said that truth is found in the intellect, and is found to the greatest degree in

God, the cause of every other being and intellect. However, as God is the cause of all things, including truth, all truth must come from him. But, as it is true that people sin, this seems to mean that sin must come from God, which is impossible.

Aquinas explains that all intellectual understanding comes from God, so the truth in the statement that (for example) a particular person commits fornication does come from God. However, the fornication itself does not come from God.

God's Will (Question XIX)

The sun shines on things, not because it wills to do so, but because that is its nature; and it is said that it is the same with God's goodness. However, voluntary agents (human beings) act as a result of reasoning and choice, so it could be argued that, if God acts by nature, not will, his will is not the cause of things.

Aquinas' response to this argument is that God's will is the cause of things, and he acts by his will, and not as a result of any necessity of his nature. This is shown in the world God has created, where both intellectual or voluntary (human) beings and natural beings act to fulfil their particular end or purpose. This is a teleological view of the universe – that even the non-rational and inanimate things in it behave in a purposeful way. Their ends (Aquinas continues) must be predetermined for them by some higher intellect, God, in the same way that an archer predetermines the flight of his arrow. As intellectual and voluntary agents are above, and precede, merely natural ones, and God is the first agent or cause, he must act by intellect and will. Further, as God's nature is un-limited, it cannot be the case that he acts by a necessity of his nature; rather, finite or limited effects, in the world he has created, proceed from his infinite perfection, according to his will and intellect.

Does God's willing something impose necessity on it, making it something that cannot not-be or happen? According to Aquinas, this is true only of some of the things God wills. This is not because of deficient secondary or intermediate causes. Nothing could stop God's will producing its intended effect in the way that he intended. If intermediate causes made the difference between something being necessary (that which cannot not-be or happen) or contingent (that which can not-be or happen), this would not involve God's intention and will, which cannot be the case. Aquinas' view is that, for the universe's perfection (so that it may contain the greatest possible variety of different kinds of things), God wills that some things happen necessarily, while others happen contingently, and thus has given some things necessary causes and others contingent ones. Therefore, things happen contingently, because God has so willed it.

Evil things happen in the world, so does God will these? Aquinas' answer is that, as good and evil are opposed, evil is not sought for itself, but only accidentally, insofar as it accompanies good. Even the fornicator does not seek sin; it is just the inevitable accompaniment of his pursuit of pleasure. The evil that accompanies one good can be seen as the privation of another good, and would not be sought, even accidentally, if the good to which it is connected were not more desired than the good of which the evil is the privation. God does not will the evil of sin, but he does will the evils of natural defect and punishment, because he wills their accompanying goods. In willing the preservation of the natural order, he wills the natural corruption of some things, and in willing justice, he wills punishment.

This argument seems both ingenious and unsatisfactory. It does not answer the question why an infinitely loving and omnipotent God, who created the world and all it contains from nothing, made it in such a way that it contains evil, with particular evils being the inevitable accompaniment of particular goods.

God's Love (Question XX)

What does it mean to say that God loves things, including human beings, and how does his love differ from that of human beings towards each other? Aquinas considers the point that, as God is only said to be angry or sorrowful in a metaphorical sense, this is also the case with love. Again, love is a passion, so how can God, who has no passions, be said to love?

Aquinas' explains that, as God has a will, he must have love. Acts of the will tend towards either good or evil, but good is its essential object and, as love does not seek good under a special condition (unlike, for example hope, which treats it as something yet to be achieved), it is naturally the first act of the will. Further, as God's will causes all things, they have being and goodness only because he wills them. So, God loves everything that exists, because to love a thing is nothing else than to will it good. And, unlike our love, which does not cause goodness, God's love creates goodness in things.

Surely, God must love all the things he has created equally? Aquinas points out that this is not the case. Things may be loved in two ways: by the act of will, and by the good a person wills for the one loved. In the first sense, God does not love one thing more than another, because he loves all things by one, simple act of his will. However, in the second sense, he has more love for those things for which he wills a greater good. And, indeed, as God's love causes goodness in things, nothing would be better than anything else, unless God willed some things more good than others. God cares for all things equally, but this does not mean he deals out equal good to all; it means that he governs all the things he has created with equal wisdom and goodness.

It seems natural to think that the better a thing is, the more God will love it, but this seems to be belied by the fact that God's love for human beings is greater than that for angels; it was for the redemption of human beings, not angels, that he gave up Jesus Christ. Aquinas rejects this interpretation. God took on human nature, and died on the cross, not because his love for human beings was greater than his love for angels, but because human need was greater.

God's Justice and Mercy (Question XXI)

As it obviously makes no sense to say that God possesses such moral virtues as temperance, which concern control of the passions (because he has no passions) does it make any more sense to say that God possesses the moral virtue of justice, particularly when he does what he wills and pleases?

Aquinas' answer is that, although moral virtues like temperance can only be applied to God metaphorically, those that relate to the will can be ascribed to him. Further, he can only will what his wisdom approves, which will always be what is right and just. Aquinas describes God's justice as 'distributive'. Like a just ruler (in his case of the whole universe), he distributes his justice to his subjects according to their deserts. His justice is present in what he has created and, by the use of their natural reason, human beings can see this in the way the universe is ordered and operates.

God is also merciful but, in God, this is not a passion, but an effect. God does not experience sorrow about human misery, in the way that human beings do about the misery of others; rather, he removes the defect of misery in human beings, whose lot, as rational beings, is to be happy. Everything God does in his creation, he does according to proper order and proportion. This is justice, but it is justice based on mercy. Nothing is due to God's creatures, except what is due to them through his goodness. God shows mercy in all that he does, giving to his creatures, from the abundance of his goodness, what is due to them more generously than they deserve.

God's Providence (Question XXII)

Aquinas tells us that providence (beneficent care) is rightly ascribed to God, who has created all the good in things, not only as concerns their substance, but also in the way they are ordered towards an end. God controls the universe he has created and, like a ruler directing his subjects, directs everything in it towards its appropriate end or purpose.

But (as with the issue of God's will) does God's providence impose necessity on things? After all, when a craftsman makes an object, he makes it as strong and stable as he can, so that it will not fail. As God is all-powerful, he could prevent failure in his creation by giving it what Aquinas calls the 'stability of necessity' – everything that happens would be something that cannot not-happen.

However, this is not the way things are – divine providence imposes necessity on some, but not all, things. Although divine providence is to do with ordering things towards an end, the principal good of all things in themselves is to perfect the universe, which involves variety. The universe is better through having all (and different) grades or levels of being, from the highest to the lowest, than if it had beings of only one kind. Therefore, the world is better through having more than one type of cause. So, some things have necessary causes, and are things that cannot not-happen, but other things have contingent causes, and are things that can not-happen.

Predestination (Question XXIII)

What about predestination – the controversial teaching that God predetermines whether people will be saved or damned, and that this is not affected by what they do in their lives? Predestination conflicts with the belief that human beings have what Aquinas refers to as 'merit and demerit' on the basis of the actions they freely choose to perform.

Aquinas explains that everything is subject to God's providence, so he does direct things towards their ends. The ultimate end of human beings is eternal life, which they cannot achieve through their own natural powers, so (just as the archer directs the arrow) God directs human beings towards eternal life; and this is called 'predestination'. However, although God loves all human beings (and, indeed, all his creatures), he does not wish all of them every good. There are those he does not wish to have eternal life, so his providence, which ordains human beings to eternal life, does include allowing some of them to fall away from that end, and this is reprobation – casting them off and denying them salvation.

Thus, while predestination causes the glory expected in the future life, and the grace received in this life, reprobation involves permitting a person to fall into sin, and then punishing him with damnation for it. However, as reprobation does not take away the power of those who are reprobated (although they are unable to acquire grace), their falling into sin comes from use of their free desire, so they are rightly held guilty for what they do. Aquinas is quite explicit that the predestination of some to eternal salvation logically presupposes that God wills their salvation, which involves both love, as he wishes these people this particular good, and election, as he selects some for salvation, in preference to others – those he reprobates.

It is difficult to find, in Aquinas' account of predestination, anything that makes this doctrine easier to understand or accept. It seems impossible to reconcile it with the Christian concept of an infinitely loving God, who cares for all his creatures, or to see how those who have been reprobated can fairly be held fully responsible for, and guilty of, their actions. However, even if we reject predestination, it does not remove the even more difficult questions of how we can reconcile the (natural and moral) evil in the world with its having been created, from nothing, by an infinitely loving and omnipotent God; or how we can reconcile belief in human freedom and responsibility with belief in God's omniscience.

Some Issues to Consider

- Aquinas maintains that, as the all-powerful creator of everything, nothing actually is remote from God, but things can be said to be remote from him in that they are unlike him in nature and grace.
- Aquinas believes there is only one God who, as his being does not depend on anything else, is supremely being; who comprehends in himself the whole perfection of being; and who maintains the order of all the diverse things that exist in the universe.

- If God is omniscient, and foreknows everything that is going to happen, is it possible to believe in human freedom?
- Is it helpful to think of evil as a privation of good, or does it suggest that the evil we encounter in the world is insubstantial and easily ignored or endured?
- Aquinas often shows that many of the problems human beings have, when thinking and talking about God, arise from the limitations and ambiguities of human language.
- Aquinas maintains that, for the perfection of the universe (so that it may contain the greatest possible variety of different kinds of things), God wills that some things happen necessarily, while others happen contingently, and thus has given some things necessary causes and others contingent ones.
- It is hard to understand why an infinitely loving and omnipotent God, who created the world and all it contains from nothing, made it in such a way that it contains evil, with particular evils being the inevitable accompaniment of particular goods.
- Aquinas believes that God's love, unlike ours, which does not cause goodness, creates goodness in things.
- Aquinas argues that God took on human nature, and died on the cross for human beings, not because he loves them more than angels, but because human need was greater.
- According to Aquinas, God's justice is present in the universe and, by using their natural reason, human beings can see this in the way it is ordered and operates.
- Aquinas holds that God's mercy is an effect, not a passion – he does not experience sorrow about human misery, as human beings do, but removes the defect of misery in human beings.
- Aquinas believes that God controls the universe he has

created, and directs everything in it towards its appropriate end or purpose.

- Aquinas explains that, although God loves all human beings, he does not wish all of them every good. There are those he does not wish to have eternal life, so his providence, which ordains human beings to eternal life, does include allowing some of them to fall away from that end.
- Reprobation does not take away the power of those who are reprobated; their falling into sin comes from use of their free desire, and so they are rightly held guilty for what they do.

Suggestions for Further Reading

Basic Writings of Saint Thomas Aquinas, vol. I, ed. A. C. Pegis, Indianapolis/Cambridge: Hackett Publishing Company (contains the *Summa Theologica*, Part I), 1997.

Basic Writings of Saint Thomas Aquinas, vol. II, ed. A. C. Pegis, Indianapolis/Cambridge: Hackett Publishing Company, 1997.

Anselm, Proslogion with the Replies of Gaunilo and Anselm, ed. T. Williams, Indianapolis/Cambridge: Hackett Publishing Company, 2001.

F. C. Copleston, *Aquinas*, Harmondsworth: Penguin, 1955.

F. C. Copleston, *A History of Philosophy*, vol. 2, Part II, New York: Image Books, 1962.

J. H. Hick, *Philosophy of Religion*, fourth edition, Englewood Cliffs, New Jersey: Prentice Hall, 1990.

A. Nichols, *Discovering Aquinas: An Introduction to His Life, Work and Influence*, London: Darton, Longman and Todd, 2002.

P. Vardy, *The Puzzle of God*, revised edition, London: Fount Paperbacks, 1999.

Detailed Summary of Thomas Aquinas'
Summa Theologica

God (Part II)

Question VIII   The Existence of God in Things

First Article   Whether God Is in all Things? (pp. 63–4)

Objection 1. **God** seems not to be 'in all things', because he is 'above all' (p. 63).

Obj. 2. What is in something is 'contained' by it, but God contains things (p. 63). He is not in things; they are in him.

Obj. 3. God is 'the most powerful of all **agents**' (p. 63). He does not need to be in 'all things', in order to affect them (p. 63).

Obj. 3. God is not 'in the **demons**', because *'light and darkness'* are opposed to each other (p. 63).

On the contrary, God 'operates in all things', and so is in them (p. 63).

I answer that, God is in all things, not as 'part of their **essence**', nor as an '**accident**', but as an 'agent' is to that on which 'it acts', who must be 'joined' to it, to act on it immediately (p. 63). God is 'being itself by His own Essence', so '**created being**' is his 'proper **effect**', and he has this effect in things as long as they remain in 'being' (pp. 63–4). Thus, he must be present to things as long as they have being, and so is 'in all things, and **innermostly**' (p. 64).

Reply Obj. 1. God, by his 'excellence', is above all things, but is in them as the **cause** of their being (p. 64).

Reply Obj. 2. Just as the '**soul** contains the body', God is 'in things as containing them' (p. 64). But we say they are in God, in that 'they are contained by Him' (p. 64).

Reply Obj. 3. God's '**supreme power**' means he 'acts immediately in all things', so nothing is remote from him, as if it was 'without God in itself' (p. 64). However, things can be said to be remote from God, because they are unlike him in '**nature** or **grace**' (p. 64).

Reply Obj. 4. Demons have a nature from God, but not their '**deformity of sin**' (p. 64). We cannot say 'absolutely' that God is in demons, except to the extent that they are '*beings*' (p. 64).

Question XI   The Unity of God

Third Article   Whether God Is One? (pp. 88–90)

Objection 1. God seems not to be one, because there are said to be '*many gods*' (1 Corinthians 8:5) (p. 88).

Obj. 2. '*One*', a number, cannot be '**predicated** of God', because it is a 'quantity', which God is not (p. 88).

On the contrary, in Deuteronomy 6:4, it states that, '*the Lord our God is one Lord*' (p. 89).

I answer that, there are three ways of showing that 'God is one' (p. 89). First, there is his '**simplicity**' (p. 89). In the same way that what makes **Socrates** 'this particular man' is 'communicable' to only one person, what makes God God belongs only to him, as he 'Himself is His own nature' (p. 89). God is 'God and this God', and so there cannot be many gods (p. 89).

Second, God 'comprehends in Himself the whole perfection of being' (p. 89). If there were many gods, they would 'necessarily differ from each other' (p. 89). One would not have something that another had. If this were a '**privation**', one would not be '**absolutely perfect**', if a '**perfection**', one would lack it (p. 89). So, there cannot be many gods. The **ancient philosophers** maintained that there was only one '**infinite principle**' (p. 89).

Third, there is the '**unity of the world**' (p. 89). Things in the world are 'ordered to each other', as some serve others (p. 89). But 'diverse' things need to be brought together 'in the same order' by 'one being' (p. 89). What is first is 'most perfect', not 'accidentally', but *'per se'* (p. 89). The first, God, who 'reduces all into one order', must be 'only one' (p. 89).

Reply Obj. 1. It was the error of those who worshipped many gods to believe there was more than one. In 1 Corinthians 8.6, **Paul** added, *'Our God is one'* (p. 89).

Reply Obj. 2. *'One'*, the 'principle of number', is predicated of '**material things**' (p. 89). One that is 'convertible with being is something **metaphysical**', and not dependent on 'matter' (p. 89). Although there is no 'privation' in God, our knowledge of him reflects our limitations, so we do apply such '**privative terms**' as *'incorporeal'* and *'infinite'* to him, and we can refer to him as *'one'* (pp. 89–90).

Fourth Article   Whether God Is Supremely One? (p. 90)

Objection 1. God is 'not supremely *one*', as this is 'so called from the privation of division', and privation 'cannot be greater or less' (p. 90). So, God is not 'more *one*' than other things called one (p. 90).

Obj. 2. Nothing seems 'more **indivisible** than what is **actually** and **potentially** indivisible', such as **unity** (p. 90). However, a thing is 'more *one* according as it is indivisible' (p. 90). So, God is not 'more *one*' than unity is (p. 90).

Obj. 3. As with good, what is 'essentially *one* is supremely *one*' (p. 90). But every being is 'essentially *one*', and so 'supremely *one*' (p. 90). Thus, God is not '*one* more than any other being' (p. 90).

On the contrary, Bernard states that the unity of the **Trinity** has first place among '*all things called one*' (p. 90).

I answer that, one is 'undivided being', so what is 'supremely *one*' is 'supremely being and supremely undivided'; and God is both (p. 90). He is supremely being, because his being is '**not determined by any nature**' to which it is attached, and 'supremely undivided', because, as he is 'altogether simple', he is not 'actually' or 'potentially' divided by any 'mode of division' (p. 90). Thus, he is '*one* in the supreme degree' (p. 90).

Reply Obj. 1. Privation is not, in itself, '**susceptive** of more or less', but its opposite is, so more or less can be predicated of privation (p. 90). Therefore, as something is 'more or less or not at all divided or divisible', to that extent, it is 'more, or less, or supremely, *one*' (p. 90).

Reply Obj. 2. Unity, the 'principle of number', is not 'supremely being', as it has being 'only in some subject'; so, it cannot be 'supremely *one*' (p. 90). As a subject cannot be supremely one, because of 'the diversity of accident and subject', neither can accident (p. 90).

Reply Obj. 3. Every being is '*one* by its **substance**', but not every substance is 'equally the cause of unity', because the substance of some things, unlike others, is '**composite**' (p. 90).

Question XIV   On God's Knowledge

Eighth Article   Whether the Knowledge of God Is the Cause of Things? (pp. 147–8)

Objection 1. God's knowledge seems not to cause things. **Origen** says that a thing happens because it is in the future, not *'because God knows it as future'* (p. 147).

Obj. 2. Effect follows cause, but God's knowledge is **eternal**. So, if God's knowledge causes 'created things', it seems they are eternal (p. 147).

Obj. 3. As **Aristotle** says, the *'knowable thing is prior to knowledge'* (p. 147). As what is '**posterior**' cannot be a cause, God's knowledge does not cause things (p. 147).

On the contrary, **Augustine** states that because God *'knows them, therefore they are'* (p. 147).

I answer that, God's knowledge does cause things, as the **artificer**'s knowledge causes things 'made by his art' (p. 147). The '**intelligible form**' in the artificer's **intellect** 'must be the **principle of action**', but only if there is 'added to it the inclination to an effect', which is 'through the will' (p. 147). The **form** would not produce 'a **determinate effect**', unless determined by the appetite (p. 147). God, by his intellect, is the cause of things, 'since His being is His act of understanding'; and his knowledge must be 'the cause of things, in so far as His will is joined to it' (p. 147).

Reply Obj. 1. Origen was referring to that 'aspect of knowledge', to which 'the idea of causality does not belong unless the will is joined to it' (p. 147).

Reply Obj. 2. God's knowledge is the cause of things, according as they are 'in His knowledge' (p. 148). However, this does not include 'that things should be eternal', so it does not follow 'that **creature**s are eternal' (p. 148).

Reply Obj. 3. **Natural things** are 'midway' between God's knowledge and ours, as we 'receive knowledge from natural things', which are caused by God, through his knowledge (p. 148). As the natural things that we can know are 'prior to our knowledge', God's knowledge 'is prior to them' (p. 148). They are like a house, which is midway between the builder's knowledge and that of a person who gets his knowledge 'from the house already built' (p. 148).

Tenth Article   Whether God Knows Evil Things? (pp. 149–50)

Objection 1. God seems not to know **evil things** because, as Aristotle says, the intellect that 'is not in potentiality does not know privation'; and, as Augustine says, *'evil is the privation of good'* (p. 149).

Obj. 2. Knowledge either causes, or is caused by, the 'thing known' (p. 149). But God's knowledge neither causes, nor is caused by, evil, so God 'does not know evil things' (p. 149).

Obj. 3. Things are known by their likeness or their opposite. God knows things 'through His essence' but, as this has 'no contrary', it is neither the likeness of, nor the contrary of, evil (p. 149). Thus, God does not know evil.

Obj. 4. Things known through something else, not themselves, are 'imperfectly known' (p. 149). Evil is not known through God, as there is no evil in God. However, if God knows evil through good, he will know it imperfectly; so, he does not know evil things.

On the contrary, 'Hell and destruction are before God' (Proverbs 15:11) (p. 150).

I answer that, knowing something perfectly is to know everything that can happen to it, and some good things can be corrupted by evil. If God did not know evil things, he 'would not know good things perfectly' (p. 150). Things are knowable to the degree in which they are. As 'the essence of evil' is to be 'privation of good', by knowing good things, God also knows evil things (p. 150).

Reply Obj. 1. Aristotle meant that an intellect that is not 'in potentiality' does not know privation through a privation of its own, but 'by its opposite, the good' (p. 150).

Reply Obj. 2. God's knowledge does not cause evil, but the good, by which 'evil is known' (p. 150).

Reply Obj. 3. Evil is not the contrary of the divine essence, but it is 'opposed' to God's effects (p. 150). God knows these 'by His essence', and so knows evil (p. 150).

Reply Obj. 4. Knowing one thing through another is imperfect knowledge, if the former is 'knowable in itself' (p. 150). But, as evil is 'privation of good', it can only be known through good (p. 150).

Question XVI   On Truth

Fifth Article   Whether God Is Truth? (p. 174)

Objection 1. God is not truth, as this requires the intellect to compose and divide but, in God, 'there is no composition or division' (p. 174).

Obj. 2. Augustine says truth is *'likeness to the source'*, but this does not apply to God (p. 174).

Obj. 3. God is 'the **first cause** of all things', and so 'of all good' (p. 174). However, if there were truth in him, all truth would 'be from Him' (p. 174). As it is true that people sin, this would then be from him, but this is 'evidently false' (p. 174).

On the contrary, Jesus says, '*I am the Way, the Truth and the Life*' (John 14:6) (p. 174).

I answer that, truth is 'found in the intellect', and this is so 'to the greatest degree' with God, who is 'the measure and cause' of every other being and every other intellect (p. 174). Not only is truth in him, but 'the highest and first truth itself' (p. 174).

Reply Obj. 1. There is no composition or division in God's intellect, but 'in His simple act of intelligence He judges of all things and knows all **propositions**' (p. 174).

Reply Obj. 2. The truth of things is their 'conformity with their source', which is the 'divine intellect' (p. 174). But this cannot be said of 'divine truth' except, perhaps, in relation to 'the **Son**, Who has a source' (p. 174). We need to put Augustine's proposition into negative form: '*the Father is of Himself, because He is not from another*' (p. 174). However, the 'divine truth' can be called '*a likeness of its source*', as God's 'being is not unlike His intellect' (p. 174).

Reply Obj. 3. All '**apprehension** of the intellect' is from God (p. 174). So, the truth in the statement, '*that this person commits fornication is true*', does come from God (p. 174). However, it is a 'fallacy of accident' to argue, '*Therefore that this person fornicates is from God*' (p. 174)

Question XIX The Will of God

Fourth Article *Whether the Will of God Is the Cause of Things? (pp. 200–1)*

Objection 1. **Dionysius** says that, just as the sun shines on things '*by its very being*', so, too, the '*divine good*' transmits its goodness to things '*by its very essence*' (p. 200). However, as **voluntary agents** act 'by reasoning and choice', if God does not act by will, his will is not the cause of things (p. 200).

Obj. 2. Further, 'the first in any order is that which is essentially so' (p. 200). As '**first agent**', God 'acts by His essence', which is his nature, not by will (p. 200).

Obj. 3. That which causes something, because it is a thing of the same kind, is a cause by nature, not will (p. 200). This is the case with God, for, as Augustine says, we exist, because '*God is good*' (p. 200).

Obj. 4. One thing has one cause. God's knowledge is the 'cause of created things', so it cannot be his will (p. 200).

On the contrary, it is written: '*How could anything endure, if Thou wouldst not?*' (Wisdom 11:26) (p. 200).

I answer that, there are three ways of showing that God's will is the cause of things, and that he acts by his will, not 'by a **necessity of His nature**' (p. 200). First, as both '*intellect and nature* act for an end', the 'natural agent must have the end and the necessary means predetermined for it by some higher intellect': as the archer predetermines the arrow's flight (pp. 200–1). As the 'intellectual and voluntary agent' must precede the natural one, and God is the first agent, he must 'act by intellect and will' (p. 201).

Second, it is the 'character of a natural agent', whose being is 'determinate', to produce the same effect, because the nature of the agent's act will always be in keeping with his nature (p. 201). However, as God's nature is 'undetermined', containing the 'full perfection of being', it cannot be the case that 'He acts by a necessity of His nature'; rather, 'determined effects proceed from His own infinite perfection according to the determination of His will and intellect' (p. 201).

Third, effects proceed from an agent 'in so far as they

pre-exist in the agent'; and they do so 'after the mode of the cause' (p. 201). As God is 'His own intellect, effects pre-exist in Him after the mode of intellect' (p. 201). They proceed from him 'after the mode of will', because his 'inclination to put in act what His intellect has conceived pertains to the will' (p. 201). Thus, God's will is the cause of things.

Reply Obj. 1. Dionysius did not intend to 'exclude **election**' (p. 201). He was suggesting that 'election implies a certain distinction', whereas God 'communicates His goodness' to all beings, not just selected ones (p. 201).

Reply Obj. 2. As God's essence is his 'intellect and will', as he acts 'by His essence, it follows that He acts after the mode of intellect and will' (p. 201).

Reply Obj. 3. Augustine's words are true, as God's goodness is the reason he wills 'all other things' (p. 201).

Reply Obj. 4. In human beings, the form of a thing to be done is conceived in the intellect, but it is the will that determines whether it is 'to exist or not exist actually'. However, 'in God all these things are one' (p. 201).

Eighth Article   Whether the Will of God Imposes Necessity on the Things Willed? (pp. 207–8)

Objection 1. Augustine says that no one is saved, *'except whom God has willed to be saved'* (p. 207). If God wills it, *'it must necessarily be'*, so God's will does impose necessity on the things willed (p. 207).

Obj. 2. Causes 'that cannot be hindered' produce their effects 'necessarily'; and God's will 'cannot be hindered' (p. 207).

Obj. 3. That which is '**necessary** by its **antecedent** cause is necessary absolutely' (p. 207). Things God has created 'are related to the divine will as to an antecedent cause', whereby they have their necessity (p. 207). Thus, the following **conditional proposition** is true: '*if God wills a thing, it comes to pass*' (p. 207).

On the contrary, God wills the existence of all good things. If God's will 'imposes necessity on the things willed', then 'all good happens of necessity', which ends **free choice** (p. 207).

I answer that, God's will imposes necessity only on 'some things willed', which some people explain by '**intermediate causes**': that 'what God produces by necessary causes is necessary' and 'what He produces by **contingent** causes contingent' (p. 208). This does not seem satisfactory. The effect of a first cause may be contingent, due to the '**secondary cause**' being deficient (p. 208). However, such a 'defect' would not stop 'God's will from producing its effect' (p. 208). Further, if the necessary and the contingent are distinguished only by reference to secondary causes, the distinction 'escapes the divine intention and will', which cannot be the case (p. 208).

It is preferable to say this occurs due to the divine will's 'efficacy' (p. 208). When a cause is 'efficacious to act', the effect 'follows upon the cause', both by being done and in the way it is done (p. 208). God wills some things to be done necessarily, others contingently, 'for the perfection of the universe'; thus, he has given some effects 'unfailing necessary causes' and others '**defectible** and contingent' ones (p. 208). Effects do not occur contingently, because their '**proximate causes** are contingent', but because God has 'willed that they should happen contingently', and so has given them contingent causes (p. 208).

Reply Obj. 1. Augustine's words must refer to a necessity in the things God wills, which is 'not absolute, but conditional', for the 'conditional proposition that *if God wills a thing, it must necessarily be*, is necessarily true' (p. 208).

Reply Obj. 2. Nothing resists God's will, so it follows that 'those things happen that God wills to happen', and that they 'happen necessarily or contingently according to His will' (p. 208).

Reply Obj. 3. Antecedents give necessity to their **consequents**, 'according to their mode' (p. 208). The things God brings about have the kind of necessity he wills for them, which may be 'absolute or conditional', so not everything is 'necessary absolutely' (p. 208).

Ninth Article   Whether God Wills Evils? (pp. 209–10)

Objection 1. God seems to will evil, because he wills all good things, and Augustine states that, '*it is good that not only good things should exist, but also evil things*' (p. 209).

Obj. 2. Augustine also says that evil adds to the beauty of the universe, as it '*commends the good the more evidently, so that the good be more pleasing*' (p. 209). As God wills everything relating to the 'perfection and beauty of the universe', he wills evil things (p. 209).

Obj. 3. That evil should exist, and that it should not, are '**contradictory** opposites' (p. 209). If God wills that evil should not exist, his will is not fulfilled, as 'various evils do exist' (p. 209). Thus, God must will the existence of evil.

On the contrary, God does not 'will that man becomes worse' (p. 209). However, evils make things worse, so God does not will evil.

I answer that, as good and evil are opposed, and we seek good, it is impossible that evil is sought by either the natural or the 'intellectual appetite which is the will' (p. 209). However, it may be 'sought accidentally, so far as it accompanies a good' (p. 209). For example, the '**fornicator**' seeks pleasure, but sin accompanies it (p. 209).

The evil accompanying one good is 'the privation of another', and would not be sought, even accidentally, if the good, to which it is connected, were not 'more desired than the good of which the evil is the privation' (p. 209). God wills 'no good more than He wills His own goodness', but he wills 'one good more than another' (pp. 209–10). He does not will the evil of sin, which is 'the privation of right order towards the divine good' (p. 210). However, he does will the evils of '**natural defect**' and punishment, because he wills the goods that go with them: in willing justice, he wills punishment and, in willing the **preservation of the natural order**, he wills the natural corruption of some things (p. 210).

Reply Obj. 1. Some have said that, although God does not will evil, he wills that it should be done because, although it is 'not a good', things that are 'evil in themselves are ordered to some good end' (p. 210). However, this is not the case, because evil only produces good accidentally. The sinner does not intend that good should flow from his sin, any more than **tyrants** intended that their persecutions should produce **martyrs** whose patience would 'shine forth' (p. 210). Nothing can be judged by what relates to it accidentally, but only by 'that which belongs to it essentially' (p. 210).

Reply Obj. 2. Evil contributes to the universe's 'perfection and beauty' only accidentally, so Dionysius' conclusion was 'the consequence of **false premises**' (p. 210).

Reply Obj. 3. While the statements that 'evil comes to be and that it does not' are contradictory, the statements that someone 'wills evil to be and that he wills it not to be', are not, as 'either is affirmative' (p. 210). God neither wills evil to be, or not to be, done; he 'wills to permit evil to be done, and this is a good' (p. 210).

Tenth Article   Whether God Has Free Choice? (pp. 210–11)

Objection 1. It seems not, for **Jerome** says that God alone is not liable to sin, whereas *'all others, as having free choice, can be inclined to either side'* (p. 210).

Obj. 2. Free choice is a 'faculty of the reason and will, by which good and evil are chosen'. God does not will evil, so there is no free choice in God (p. 210).

On the contrary, according to **Ambrose**, the *'Holy Spirit divideth unto each one as He will . . . according to the free choice of the will'* (p. 210).

I answer that, human beings have free choice in relation to what they do not will 'of necessity, or by natural instinct', but the latter moves other animals to action, so they do not (p. 211). As God 'wills his own goodness necessarily', but not other things, he has free choice in relation to them (p. 211).

Reply Obj. 1. This does not deny that God has free choice absolutely, but not in relation to 'turning to sin' (p. 211).

Reply Obj. 2. As sin involves 'turning away from the divine goodness', by which God 'wills all things', it is not possible for him to will sin (p. 211). But, he can choose 'one of two opposites', such that he can will something to be or not to be (p. 211).

Question XX   God's Love

First Article   Whether Love Exists in God? (pp. 215–17)

Objection 1. As **love** is a **passion**, and God has no passions, love seems not to 'exist in God' (p. 215).

Obj. 2. Sorrow and anger are not ascribed to God, except 'by **metaphor**', so neither is love (p. 215).

Obj. 3. Dionysius describes love as '*a uniting and binding force*', but this cannot be the case with God, who 'is simple' (p. 215).

On the contrary, '*God is love*' (1 John 4:16) (p. 215).

I answer that, there must be love in God, as it is 'the first movement of the will' (p. 215). Acts of will 'tend towards good and evil as to their proper objects' (p. 215). However, good is the will's object 'essentially and especially'; evil only 'secondarily and indirectly' (p. 215). Thus, acts of the will related to good are naturally 'prior to those that regard evil' (p. 215).

What is more, universal is 'prior' to what is less so (p. 215). Thus, the 'intellect' is directed first to 'universal truth', then to 'particular' truths (pp. 215–16). Now, there are acts of will which 'regard good under some special condition', as with hope, which regards it as not 'yet possessed' (p. 216). But love 'regards good universally', and so is 'naturally the first act of will': nobody desires or rejoices in anything, 'except as a good that is loved' (p. 216). So, where there is a will, there must be love, too; and, as God has a will, he must have love.

Reply Obj. 1. The will moves 'through the medium of the **sensitive appetite**', which is the 'proximate motive-power of our bodies' (p. 216). An 'act of the sensitive appetite' is always accompanied by 'bodily change', which affects the heart, animals' 'first source of movement' (p. 216). Acts of the sensitive appetite are called 'passions'; acts of the will are not (p. 216). To the extent that it denotes an act of the sensitive appetite, love is a passion, but not to the extent that it is an act of the **'intellective appetite'**; and it is in this latter sense that it is in God (p. 216).

Reply Obj. 2. In passions of the sensitive appetite, there is a **'material element'** (in anger, for example, 'surging of the blood') and a **'formal element'** (the 'appetite for revenge' in anger) (p. 216). Further, an 'imperfection' is implied in the 'formal element' of many passions: anger implies 'sorrow' (p. 216). However, other passions, like love, 'imply no imperfection' (p. 216). The material element and the imperfection in the formal element in passions cannot be 'attributed to God', but love can properly be 'predicated of God', but without ascribing passion to him (pp. 216–17).

Reply Obj. 3. An act of love tends towards 'the good that one wills' and the person 'for whom one wills it', as to love someone is to will 'good for that person' (p. 217). Insofar as we 'love ourselves', we will ourselves good and 'union with that good' (p. 217). So, love is a **unitive force**, even in God, although this does not imply 'composition' in God (p. 217). To love another is to put him in one's own place, and consider the 'good done to him' as done to oneself (p. 217). Thus, love is a 'binding force', joining another to ourselves, and referring 'his good to our own' (p. 217). And so, too, is the **divine love**, as God wills good to others, but, again, this implies no composition in him (p. 217).

Second Article   Whether God Loves All Things? (pp. 217–18)

Objection 1. God does not love all things because, according to Dionysius, love causes the lover to pass 'into the object of his love' (p. 217). However, God does not pass 'into other things', so it cannot be said that God loves things other than himself (p. 217).

Obj. 2. God's love is 'eternal', but other things are only eternal in God. Thus, God only loves things as they exist in him; but, if things exist in God, they are 'no other than Himself' (p. 217).

Obj. 3. There are two kinds of love: 'of desire' and 'of friendship' (p. 217). God does not have the first kind of love for '**irrational creatures**', because he 'needs no creature outside Himself', nor can he have friendship with them (p. 217).

Obj. 4. In Psalm 5:7, it says God hates all '*workers of iniquity*' (p. 217). As something cannot be loved and hated at the same time, 'God does not love all things' (p. 217).

On the contrary, in Wisdom 11:25, it states that God loves '*all things that are*', and hates none of the things he made (p. 217).

I answer that, God's will is 'the cause of all things', so they have being and goodness, 'only inasmuch as it is willed by God' (pp. 217–18). So, God loves 'everything that exists', because to love a thing is 'nothing else than to will good' to it (p. 218). And, unlike ours, which is not 'the cause of the goodness of things', God's love '**infuses** and creates goodness in things' (p. 218).

Reply Obj. 1. A lover passes 'into the object of his love', insofar as he 'wills good to the beloved', and works for its good as for his own (p. 218).

Reply Obj. 2. Creatures have not 'existed from eternity, except in God', but, as they have been in him from eternity, God has known, and loved, them 'eternally in their proper natures' (p. 218).

Reply Obj. 3. Friendship exists only towards **rational creatures**, 'capable of returning love and of communicating with one another'; so, 'irrational creatures cannot attain to loving God' (p. 218). God's love for irrational creatures is that of desire, in that he 'orders them to rational creatures, and even to Himself': not because he needs them, but 'because of His goodness' (p. 218).

Reply Obj. 4. Something can be loved in one respect, and hated in another. God loves sinners as 'existing natures', because they are from him (p. 218). But, as sinners, they are not from him, and he hates them 'under this aspect' (p. 218).

Third Article   Whether God Loves All Things Equally? (p. 219)

Objection 1. God seems to love 'all things equally', as '*He hath equally care of all*' (Wisdom 6:8) (p. 219).

Obj. 2. God's love 'is His essence', but this does 'not admit of degree', so he does not 'love some things more than others' (p. 219).

Obj. 3. God is not said to know or will 'some things more than others', and this is also the case with his love (p. 219).

On the contrary, Augustine says that God loves '*rational creatures more*'; of these, '*especially those who are members of **His only-begotten son**'*; and his son '*more than all*' (p. 219).

I answer that, things may be loved in two ways: by the act of will, which is 'more or less intense', and by the good that a person wills for the one loved (p. 219). In the first way, God does not love one thing more than another, because he loves all things by one, simple 'act of the will' (p. 219). However, in the second way, he has more love for those things for which he wills 'a greater good' (p. 219). As God's love is 'the cause of goodness in things', nothing would be better than anything else, if God did not will some things 'greater good' (p. 219).

Reply Obj. 1. God cares for all things equally, not by dealing out 'equal good to all', but by governing all things with equal 'wisdom and goodness' (p. 219).

Reply Obj. 2. The good God wills 'for His creatures is not the divine essence', and so may vary (p. 219).

Reply Obj. 3. Understanding and willing 'signify only acts'

(p. 219). They do not 'include in their meaning objects from the diversity of which God may be said to know or will more or less' (p. 219).

Fourth Article   Whether God Always Loves Better Things More? (pp. 220–2)

Objection 1. God does not 'love better things more', for **Christ** was 'better than the whole human race', but God loved the human race more than Christ, as he *'delivered Him up for us all'* (Romans 8:32) (p. 220).

Obj. 2. **Angels** are better than human beings, but God loves them more than angels, because it is not angels, but *'of the seed of Abraham He taketh hold'* (Hebrews 2:16) (p. 220).

Obj. 3. **Peter** was 'better than **John**, since he loved Christ more', but Christ 'loved John more than He loved Peter' (p. 220).

Obj. 4. The '**innocent** man is better than the **repentant**', but God loves the repentant one more, as 'He rejoices over him the more' (p. 220).

Obj. 5. God loves 'the **predestined** sinner' more than 'the **just** man who is merely **foreknown**' (although the latter is better than the former), since he wills him 'a greater good, namely, **life eternal**' (p. 220).

On the contrary, the more like God something is, the better it is; so 'better things are more loved by God' (p. 220).

I answer that, God does love better things more. God's will causes goodness in things, and his loving some things more than others is his willing for them 'a greater good'; and this is why 'some things are better than others' (pp. 220–1).

Reply Obj. 1. God loves Christ more than 'the entire created universe', and 'by God's will Christ was true God' (p. 221). Christ's 'excellence' was not diminished when God delivered him up to die 'for the **salvation of the human race**'; rather, he became 'thereby a glorious conqueror' (p. 221).

Reply Obj. 2. God loves 'the **human nature assumed by the Word of God in the person of Christ**' more than the angels: that nature is better, due to '**union with the Godhead**' (p. 221). In general, human and angelic nature are 'equal in the order of grace' although, in 'the condition of their natures', angels are better than men (p. 221). God took on human nature, not because he 'loved man more, but because the needs of man were greater' (p. 221).

Reply Obj. 3. Augustine says that Peter's '**active life**' shows more love for God than John's '**contemplative life**', because it indicates greater awareness of 'the miseries of this present life', and a stronger desire to break free of them, and 'reach God' (p. 221). However, God loves the contemplative life more, as it does not end when 'the life of the body' does (p. 221). Some say that Peter's love for Christ, as an active follower, was greater, which was why he was given '**care of the Church**', but that John loved Christ more 'in Himself', which was why he was entrusted with the **care of Christ's mother** (p. 221). Other views are that it is uncertain which of the two God loved more; that Peter was loved more for his 'promptness and fervor', while John was preferred for his 'youth and purity'; and that Christ loved Peter more for his 'more excellent **gift of charity**', but John more for his 'gifts of intellect' (p. 221).

Reply Obj. 4. Whether innocent or penitent, 'those are the better and the better loved who have more grace' (p. 222). All else being equal, innocence is 'nobler' and 'more beloved' (p. 222). However, God is said to rejoice more over the penitent, because he rises from sin 'more cautious, humble, and fervent' (p. 222). It could be said that 'an equal gift of grace' means more to the penitent sinner than the innocent, just as a gift of a large sum of money means more to a poor person than a rich one (p. 222).

Reply Obj. 5. God's will is 'the cause of goodness in things', so the goodness of one God loves is calculated 'according to the time when some good is given to him' (p. 222). At the time when God gives a 'greater good' to the predestined sinner, he is better than 'the innocent man' but, at other times, the opposite is the case; and there is a time 'when he is neither good nor bad' (p. 222).

Question XXI The Justice and Mercy of God

First Article   Whether there Is Justice in God? (pp. 223–5)

Objection 1. There seems not to be justice in God, because 'justice and **temperance** are divided as members of the same class' (p. 223). As the latter does not exist in God, neither does the former.

Obj. 2. One who 'does whatsoever he wills and pleases' does not operate 'according to justice', so it does not exist in God (p. 223).

Obj. 3. Justice is paying what is due, but God is 'no man's debtor' (p. 223).

Obj. 4. What is in God is 'His essence' but, according to **Boethius**, justice, unlike good, refers '*to the act*', not the essence (p. 223).

On the contrary, Psalm 10:8 states that God is just and '*hath loved justice*' (p. 223).

I answer that, there are 'two kinds of justice' (p. 223). The first, which Aristotle calls '*commutative justice*', and which does not relate to God, is concerned with 'mutual giving and receiving', and applies to business activities (p. 223). The

35

second, *'distributive justice'*, concerns, for example, a ruler's just distribution to his subjects of what each 'deserves' (p. 223). And this kind of justice is present in 'the **order of the universe'**, which 'shows forth the justice of God' (pp. 223–4). As Dionysius says, *'God is truly just, in seeing how He gives to all existing things what is proper to the condition of each'* (p. 224).

Reply Obj. 1. Some '**moral virtues** are concerned with the passions', as temperance is with '**concupiscence**' (p. 224). As there are no passions in God, such **virtues** are ascribed to him 'only metaphorically' (p. 224). Other moral virtues, such as justice, relate to 'giving' and concern 'the will' (p. 224). These virtues can be ascribed to God 'in such acts as befit Him' (p. 224).

Reply Obj. 2. God can only will 'what His wisdom approves', because it is 'His law of justice, in accordance with which His will is right and just' (p. 224). What he does according to his will, he 'does justly', as we do, when we act 'according to law' (p. 224). However, our law comes from 'some higher power', but God is 'a law unto Himself' (p. 224).

Reply Obj. 3. In things, there is 'a twofold order': one in which created things are ordained to each other, the other in which 'all created things are ordered to God' (p. 224). In 'divine operations', a debt may be due to God or creatures, but 'either way God pays what is due' (p. 224). He has 'a debt to Himself that there should be fulfilled in creatures what His will and wisdom contain', which will show his goodness (p. 224). Here, God's justice is giving himself his due. There is also a debt to creatures: that they should have 'what is ordered' to them (p. 224). In this context, God is just when he gives each thing its due, 'according to its nature and condition' (p. 224). The second kind of debt derives from the first, as each thing is due what God's wisdom orders to it (p. 224). But God is not a debtor, because 'He is not ordered to other things'; rather, his justice is 'the fitting accompaniment of His goodness' (p. 224).

Reply Obj. 4. Justice relates to acts, but this does not stop it being 'the essence of God', for something's essence may be 'a principle of action' (p. 224). Good does not always relate to acts, as something is also good 'with respect to the perfection in its essence' (p. 224). Thus, the relation of the good to the just is that of 'the general to the special' (p. 224).

Third Article   Whether Mercy Can Be Attributed to God? (pp. 226–7)

Objection 1. **Mercy** cannot be ascribed to God, as it is 'a kind of sorrow', of which there is none in God (p. 226).

Obj. 2. Mercy is 'not becoming to God', because it is 'relaxation of justice', and God does not do so (p. 226).

On the contrary, 'He is a merciful and gracious Lord' (Psalm 110:4) (p. 226).

I answer that, mercy can be ascribed to God, but 'in its effect', not as 'an **affection of passion**' (p. 226). God does not feel sorrow 'over the misery of others'; rather, he dispels 'the **defect** we call misery' (p. 226). A defect is removed by 'the perfection of some kind of goodness', of which God is the 'primary source' (p. 226).

Bestowing perfections on things belongs to God's 'justice, **liberality** and mercy', as well as his goodness (p. 226). Giving perfections to things relates to his goodness, but also to his justice, as the perfections are given in accordance with what is due to things (p. 226). As God gives perfections from goodness, and not for his own use, 'it belongs to liberality'; and as they 'expel defects, it belongs to mercy' (p. 226).

Reply Obj. 1. The argument is based on mercy as 'an affection of passion' (p. 227).

Reply Obj. 2. God 'acts mercifully', not by going against, but by exceeding, his justice, as when a man 'pardons an offense committed against him' (p. 227). Mercy does not undermine justice, but 'is the fulness thereof' (p. 227).

Fourth Article   Whether in Every Work of God there Are Mercy and Justice? (pp. 227–8)

Objection 1. It seems not, for some of God's works, such as the **justification of sinners**, are put down to mercy, while others, such as '**damnation** of the wicked', are put down to justice (p. 227).

Obj. 2. Paul (Romans 15:8) says that the Jews were converted through justice, but the **Gentiles** through mercy (p. 227).

Obj. 3. The world contains many '**afflicted' persons**, which is unjust, indicating that justice and mercy are not found in all God's works (p. 227).

Obj. 4. Justice concerns paying what is due, but mercy concerns relieving misery, so both 'presuppose something'; but creation presupposes nothing, and mercy and justice are not found in it (p. 227).

On the contrary, 'All the ways of the Lord are mercy and truth' (Psalm 24:10) (p. 227).

I answer that, both are found in 'all God's works', as long as mercy means 'removal of any kind of defect': specifically, that in 'a **rational nature** whose lot is to be happy'; and 'misery is opposed to happiness' (p. 227). Again, whatever God does 'in created things', he does 'according to proper order and proportion', which is the 'nature of justice', and which exists in 'all God's works' (pp. 227–8). Divine justice presupposes, and is based on, mercy. Nothing is due to creatures, except 'on the supposition of something already existing or already known in them' (for example, a rational soul is due to human beings, so that they may be human beings); and this must be 'because of something that precedes' (p. 228). As it is not possible to go to infinity, this must be something 'that depends only on the goodness of the divine will': the 'ultimate end' (p. 228). In all God's works, there is mercy, and, out of the 'abundance of His goodness', God bestows on creatures 'what is due to them **more bountifully than is proportionate to their deserts**' (p. 228). Less than God gives would be adequate for 'preserving the order of justice', and there is 'no proportion' between creatures and God's goodness (p. 228).

Reply Obj. 1. In some of God's works, justice 'appears more forcibly' than mercy; in other works, it is the other way round.

Reply Obj. 2. Both justice and mercy appear in both conversions. However, the element of justice in the conversion of the Jews is that they were saved, due to '**promises made to their fathers**' (p. 228).

Reply Obj. 3. Justice and mercy are present in the punishment of the just, as their 'lesser faults are cleansed', and they are brought closer to God (p. 228).

Reply Obj. 4. Although creation 'presupposes nothing in the universe', it does in God's knowledge. In this way, justice 'is preserved in creation' (p. 228). Things are 'brought into being' in a way that is in line with God's wisdom and goodness, and mercy is present in the '**transition of creatures from non-being to being**' (p. 228).

Question XXII   The Providence of God

First Article   Whether Providence Can Suitably Be Attributed to God? (pp. 229–31)

Objection 1. **Providence** does not belong to God; it is 'a part of **prudence**', which is giving 'good counsel', and God does not require counsel (p. 229).

Obj. 2. What is in God is 'eternal', but providence concerns *'existing things'* (p. 229).

Obj. 3. Providence seems 'composite', as it concerns both intellect and will, but God is not composite (p. 229).

On the contrary, God *'governeth all things by providence'* (Wisdom 14:3) (p. 229).

I answer that, providence must be ascribed to God, as he has created 'all the good that is in things' (pp. 229–30). The goodness of things relates not only to 'their substance', but to their being ordered towards an end (p. 230). As God is the cause of all things, 'the **exemplar** of the order of things towards their end' necessarily pre-exists 'in the divine mind'; and this is providence (p. 230). It is the principal part of prudence, which comprises, in addition, recollection of the past and understanding of the present; and these enable us to 'provide for the future' (p. 230). According to Aristotle, prudence is directing *'things towards an end'*, either for oneself or others, as a ruler does for his subjects (p. 230). And, in this second sense, it may be ascribed to God for, in relation to God, nothing can be '**ordainable towards an end**, since He is the last end' (p. 230). In God, providence is the 'very exemplar of the order of things towards an end' (p. 230).

Reply Obj. 1. Taking counsel does not belong to God, but giving commands for 'the ordering of things towards an end', for the right reason, does (p. 230). Thus, 'both prudence and providence belong to God' (p. 230).

Reply Obj. 2. Two things relate to providence: 'the *exemplar of order*' ('providence and disposition'), which is 'eternal', and 'the *execution of order*' ('government'), which is '**temporal**' (p. 230).

Reply Obj. 3. Providence is based in the 'intellect', but requires the 'act of willing the end' (p. 231). Similarly, prudence 'presupposes the moral virtues', by which 'the appetitive power is directed towards good' (p. 231). However, it would not 'affect the divine simplicity', even if providence related to both 'divine will and intellect', as they are the same thing in God (p. 231).

Fourth Article   Whether Providence Imposes Any Necessity on what It Foresees? (pp. 236–7)

Objection 1. Divine providence seems to impose 'necessity upon what it foresees', because effects with 'essential' causes, which they follow necessarily, come to be 'of necessity' (p. 236). God's providence is eternal, and 'precedes its effect', which necessarily 'flows from it' (p. 236).

Obj. 2. Every 'provider' renders 'his work as stable' as possible, to prevent failure (p. 236). As God is 'most powerful', he gives things 'the stability of necessity' (p. 236).

Obj. 3. Boethius writes that '*Fate from the **immutable** source of providence binds together human acts and fortunes by the indissoluble connexion of causes*'; so, providence appears to involve necessity (p. 236).

On the contrary, some things are contingent in their nature, and divine providence does not 'destroy their contingency' by imposing necessity on them (p. 236).

I answer that, divine providence imposes necessity on some, but not all, things. Providence concerns ordering things 'towards an end' (p. 236). Apart from 'divine goodness', an **'extrinsic end** to all things', their 'principal good', in themselves, is to perfect the universe; and this involves it having **'all grades of being'** (p. 236). Therefore, some things have necessary causes, other things contingent causes, depending upon their 'proximate causes' (p. 236).

Reply Obj. 1. Divine providence only requires that things 'happen *somehow*', not that they happen only 'by necessity' (p. 236). So, it orders that some things happen 'of necessity', and other things 'contingently' (p. 236).

Reply Obj. 2. The 'order of divine providence is unchangeable and certain', and all things happen as foreseen, whether necessarily or contingently (p. 236).

Reply Obj. 3. Boethius is referring to providence's 'certainty'; it always produces its effect, but not always 'by necessity' and 'necessity and contingency' (p. 237). The modes of 'necessity and contingency' are both 'consequent upon being' and come under God's foresight, which provides for all being, not just that of 'causes that provide only for **some particular order of things'** (p. 237).

Question XXIII   Predestination

First Article   *Whether Men Are Predestined by God?* *(pp. 238–40)*

Objection 1. Merit and demerit are in us as 'masters of our own acts by free choice', so they are not 'predestined by God' (p. 239).

Obj. 2. All creatures are 'directed to their ends by divine providence' (p. 238). However, 'other creatures are not said to be predestined', so human beings are not (p. 238).

Obj. 3. Angels, as well as human beings, are 'capable of **beatitude**', but predestination does not 'befit' them, as they were never unhappy, so human beings are not predestined (p. 239).

Obj. 4. The '**Holy Ghost**' **reveals** 'the benefits God confers upon men' to those who are '**holy**' (p. 239). If human beings were predestined, it would be revealed to all those predestined (p. 239).

On the contrary, Paul writes: '*Whom He predestined, them He also called*' (Romans 8:30) (p. 239).

I answer that, as everything is 'subject to His providence', God does direct things towards their ends (p. 239). A rational creature has a 'twofold' end (p. 239). One it can achieve through 'the power of its nature', but the other is beyond its ability: 'life eternal, consisting in the **vision of God**' (p. 239). If a thing cannot achieve something through its own power, it needs to be 'directed thereto', as an arrow is by an archer; and God directs rational creatures towards **eternal life** (p. 239). The '**exemplar of that direction pre-exists in God**', and, when the exemplar of 'something to be done' is in the doer's mind, it is a sort of pre-existence of what is to be done (p. 239). The exemplar of rational creatures' direction towards eternal life 'is called predestination', and it is 'part of providence' (p. 239).

Reply Obj. 1. Predestination is 'an imposition of necessity after the manner of natural things which are predetermined towards one end' (p. 239).

Reply Obj. 2. Irrational creatures lack 'the capacity for that end which exceeds the ability of human nature' (p. 239).

Reply Obj. 3. Predestination applies to angels, even though they have not been unhappy, for it makes no difference whether or not one is predestined to eternal life from 'a state of misery' (pp. 239–40).

Reply Obj. 4. Even if it were revealed to some, predestination cannot be revealed to all, as it might cause despair in those not predestined, and complacency in those who were.

Third Article   Whether God Reprobates Any Man? *(pp. 241–3)*

Objection 1. It seems not, for God 'loves every man', and no one '**reprobates**' what he loves (p. 241).

Obj. 2. If God did, reprobation would have to relate to the reprobate as predestination does to the predestined. However, predestination causes 'the salvation of the predestined', which would make reprobation the 'cause of the loss of the reprobate'; but this cannot be so (p. 242).

Obj. 3. Nothing, 'which he cannot avoid', should be imposed on anyone but, if God reprobated anyone, he would be bound to perish (p. 242).

On the contrary, 'I have loved **Jacob**, but have hated **Esau**' (Malachi 1:2–3) (p. 242).

I answer that, predestination is part of providence, and this involves allowing some defects in things subject to it. God's providence ordains human beings to eternal life, and this includes permitting some 'to fall away from that end' (p. 242). This is *'reprobation'*, which is 'part of providence in regard to those who turn aside from that end' (p. 242). Just as predestination includes 'the will to confer grace and glory', reprobation includes 'the will to permit a person to fall into sin', and to punish them with 'damnation' because of it (p. 242).

Reply Obj. 1. Although God loves 'all men and all creatures', he does not wish all of them 'every good', and is said to reprobate those whom he does not wish to have eternal life (p. 242).

Reply Obj. 2. Predestination causes the glory that is 'expected in the future life' and the grace 'received in this life' (p. 242). Reprobation does not cause present sin, but does cause 'abandonment by God' and 'eternal punishment' (p. 242). However, *'guilt proceeds from the free choice of the person who is reprobated'* (p. 242).

Reply Obj. 3. Reprobation does not take away from the reprobated person's power. It is not absolutely, but only conditionally, impossible for a reprobated person to 'obtain grace' (p. 242). Although he cannot 'acquire grace', his falling into sin 'comes from the use of his free desire', so guilt is rightly 'imputed to him' (p. 242).

Fourth Article   Whether the Predestined Are Elected by God? (pp. 243–4)

Objection 1. It seems not, for, in the same way that the sun shines on all 'without selection', so does God's goodness (p. 243).

Obj. 2. Election is of 'things that exist', but predestination 'from all eternity' is also of things that do not. So, some are 'predestined without election' (p. 243).

Obj. 3. Election 'implies some discrimination', but God 'wills all men to be saved' (1 Timothy 2:4), so there is no election in predestination (p. 243).

On the contrary, 'He chooses us in Him before the foundation of the world' (Ephesians 1:4) (p. 243).

I answer that, predestination 'logically presupposes election', which presupposes love (p. 243). The predestination of some to '**eternal salvation** logically presupposes that God wills their salvation', which involves both love (he wishes them 'this particular good') and election (he wills it for some, 'in preference to others', since he 'reprobates some') (p. 243). Election and love are not ordered in God in the same way as they are in us. In us, the will to love 'does not cause good'; rather, we are led to love by an already existing good (p. 243). It is the other way with God. His will, 'by which in loving He wishes good to someone', causes that good that some possess 'in preference to others' (pp. 243–4). Logically, love 'precedes election', which precedes predestination (p. 244).

Reply Obj. 1. God communicates his goodness without election, in the sense that all things 'share in His goodness' (p. 244). But he uses election when communicating particular goods, as he gives certain ones to some, but not others.

Reply Obj. 2. We choose the existing good in things that already exist, but this does not apply to God who, as Augustine states, chooses those *'who do not exist; yet He does not err in His choice'* (p. 244).

Reply Obj. 3. God wills that all men be saved 'by His antecedent will', which is 'to will, not absolutely, but relatively; and not by His consequent will, which is to will absolutely' (p. 244).

Overview

The following section is a chapter-by-chapter overview of Aquinas' *Summa Theologica* (God, Part II), designed for quick reference to the detailed summary above. Readers may also find this section helpful for revision.

God (Part II)

Question VIII   The Existence of God in Things

First Article   Whether God Is in all Things? (pp. 63–4)

The objections are:

- God seems not to be in all things, because he is above all;
- what is in something is contained by it, but God contains things;
- God is the most powerful agent, and does not need to be in all things, to affect them;
- God is not in demons, as light and darkness are opposed to each other.

Aquinas' answer is: God is in all things, not as part of their essence or as an accident, but as an agent to that on which it acts, and which must be joined to it, to act on it immediately. By his essence, God is being itself, so created being is his proper effect, which he has in things as long as they remain in being. He must be present to things as long as they have being, and so is in all things in an innermost way.

His replies to the objections are:

- God is above all things, but is in them as the cause of their being;

- as the soul contains the body, God is in things, containing them, but we say they are in God, in that they are contained by him;
- God's supreme power means he acts immediately in all things, so nothing is remote from him, but things can be said to be remote from God, because they are unlike him in nature or grace;
- demons have a nature from God, but not their sin, so it cannot be said absolutely that God is in them, except insofar as they are beings.

Question XI   The Unity of God

Third Article   Whether God Is One? (pp. 88–90)

The objections are:

- God seems not to be one, as there are said to be many gods;
- one, a number, cannot be predicated of God, as it is a quantity, but God is not.

Aquinas' answer is: There are three ways to show God is one: he is simple, and what makes him God belongs only to him; he comprehends in himself the whole perfection of being and, if there were many gods, they would necessarily differ from each other, as one would lack something another had; things in the world are ordered to each other, as some serve others, but one being is needed to bring diverse things together in the same order, so God, who reduces all things into one order, must be one.

His replies to the objections are:

- those who worshipped many gods were wrong to believe there was more than one;

- one, the principle of number, is predicated of material things, but the one that is convertible with being is metaphysical, and not dependent on matter – although there is no privation in God, our limited knowledge of him means we apply privative terms, like 'incorporeal' and 'infinite' to him, and can refer to him as 'one'.

Fourth Article   Whether God Is Supremely One? (p. 90)

The objections are:

- God is not supremely one, as this relates to the privation of division and, as privation cannot be greater or less, God is not more one than other things called one;
- nothing seems more indivisible than what is actually and potentially indivisible, such as unity, but a thing is more one according as it is indivisible, so God is not more one than unity is;
- as with good, what is essentially one is supremely one, but every being is essentially, and so supremely, one, so God is not one more than any other being.

Aquinas' answer is: One is undivided being, so what is supremely one is supremely being and supremely undivided; and God is both. He is supremely being, because his being is not determined by any nature to which it is attached, and supremely undivided because, as he is altogether simple, he is not actually or potentially divided by any mode of division.

His replies to the objections are:

- privation is not, in itself, susceptive of more or less, but its opposite is, so more or less can be predicated of privation – as something is more or less or not at all divided or divisible, to that extent, it is more, or less, or supremely, one;

- unity, the principle of number, is not supremely being, as it has being only in a subject so, it cannot be supremely one – as a subject cannot be supremely one, because of the diversity of accident and subject, neither can accident;
- every being is one by its substance, but not every substance is equally the cause of unity, because some things have a composite substance.

Question XIV   On God's Knowledge

Eighth Article   Whether the Knowledge of God Is the Cause of Things? (pp. 147–8)

The objections are:

- God's knowledge seems not to cause things, as a thing happens because it is in the future, not because God knows it as future;
- effect follows cause, but God's knowledge is eternal so, if God's knowledge causes created things, they seem to be eternal;
- the knowable thing is prior to knowledge and, as what is posterior cannot be a cause, God's knowledge does not cause things.

Aquinas' answer is: God's knowledge does cause things, as the artificer's knowledge does. The intelligible form in the artificer's mind must be the principle of action, but only if an inclination to produce an effect is added to it, and this comes through the will. God, by his intellect, is the cause of things, since his being is his act of understanding; and his knowledge must be the cause of things, insofar as his will is joined to it.

His replies to the objections are:

- this refers to that aspect of knowledge, to which the idea of causality does not belong, unless the will is joined to it;
- God's knowledge causes things, according as they are in his knowledge, but this does not include that things should be eternal, so it does not follow that creatures are;
- natural things are midway between God's knowledge and ours, as we receive knowledge from natural things, which are caused by God, through his knowledge and, just as the natural things we can know are prior to our knowledge, God's knowledge is prior to them. They are like a house, which is midway between the builder's knowledge and that of a person who gets his knowledge from a house already built.

Tenth Article   Whether God Knows Evil Things? *(pp. 149–50)*

The objections are:

- God seems not to know evil things, because the intellect that is not in potentiality does not know privation, and evil is privation of good;
- knowledge causes, or is caused by, the thing known, but God's knowledge neither causes, nor is caused by, evil, so he does not know evil things;
- things are known by their likeness or their opposite – God knows things through his essence but, as this has no contrary, it is neither the likeness of, nor the contrary of, evil, so God does not know evil;
- things known through something else, not themselves, are imperfectly known, and evil is not known through God, as

51

there is no evil in God, but, if God knows evil through good, he will know it imperfectly.

Aquinas' answer is: Knowing something perfectly is to know everything that can happen to it, and some good things can be corrupted by evil. If God did not know evil things, he would not know good things perfectly. Things are knowable to the degree in which they are. As the essence of evil is to be privation of good, by knowing good things, God also knows evil things.

His replies to the objections are:

- an intellect that is not in potentiality does not know privation through a privation of its own, but by its opposite, the good;
- God's knowledge does not cause evil, but the good, by which evil is known;
- evil is not the contrary of the divine essence, but it is opposed to God's effects, which God knows by his essence, and so knows evil;
- knowing one thing through another is imperfect knowledge, if the former is knowable in itself, but, as evil is privation of good, it can only be known through good.

Question XVI   On Truth

Fifth Article   Whether God Is Truth? (p. 174)

The objections are:

- God is not truth, as this requires the intellect to compose and divide, but there is no composition or division in God;
- truth is said to be likeness to the source, but this does not apply to God;

- God is the first cause of all things, and so of all good but, if there were truth in him, all truth would be from him, and, as it is true that people sin, this would be from him, which cannot be so.

Aquinas' answer is: Truth is found in the intellect, and to the greatest degree in God, the measure and cause of every other being and intellect. The highest and first truth are in him.

His replies to the objections are:

- there is no composition or division in God's intellect but, in his simple act of intelligence, he judges all things and knows all propositions;
- the truth of things is their conformity with their source, which is the divine intellect, but this cannot be said of divine truth, except perhaps, in relation to Christ. However, the divine truth can be called a likeness of source, as God's being is not unlike his intellect;
- all understanding by the intellect comes from God, so the truth in the statement that it is true that a person commits fornication comes from God, but it is wrong to argue that the fornicating itself comes from God.

Question XIX   The Will of God

Fourth Article   Whether the Will of God Is the Cause of Things (pp. 200–1)

The objections are:

- as the sun shines on things by its very being, the divine good transmits its goodness to things by its very essence, but voluntary agents act by reasoning and choice so, if God acts by nature, not will, his will is not the cause of things;

- the first in any order is that which is essentially so and, as first agent, God acts by his essence, which is his nature, not by will;
- what causes something, because it is a thing of the same kind, is a cause by nature, not will, and this is the case with God – we exist, because he is good;
- one thing has one cause and, as God's knowledge causes created things, it cannot be his will.

Aquinas' answer is: There are three ways of showing that God's will is the cause of things, and that he acts by his will, not a necessity of nature. First, as both intellect and nature act for an end, the natural agent must have the end and the necessary means predetermined for it by some higher intellect – as the archer predetermines the arrow's flight. As the intellectual and voluntary agent must precede the natural one, and God is the first agent, he must act by intellect and will. Second, it is a natural agent's character, having limited being, to produce the same effect, because the nature of the agent's act will always be in keeping with his nature. However, as God's nature is unlimited, it cannot be the case that he acts by a necessity of nature; rather, finite effects proceed from his own infinite perfection, according to his will and intellect. Third, effects proceed from an agent, insofar as they pre-exist in the agent, and they do so after the mode of the cause. As God is his own intellect, effects pre-exist in him after the mode of intellect. They proceed from him after the mode of will, because his inclination to put into effect what he has conceived in his intellect relates to the will. Thus, God's will is the cause of things.

His replies to the objections are:

- this does not exclude selection, but suggests that it implies a certain distinction, whereas God communicates his goodness to all beings, not just selected ones;
- as God's essence is his intellect and will, it follows that, as he acts by his essence, he acts after the mode of intellect and will;
- this is true, as God's goodness is the reason he wills all other things;
- in human beings, the form of a thing to be done is conceived in the intellect, but the will determines whether or not it exists actually, but in God these things are one.

Eighth Article   Whether the Will of God Imposes Necessity on the Things Willed? (pp. 207–8)

The objections are:

- no one is saved, unless God has willed it and, as what God wills must necessarily be, God's will does impose necessity on the things willed;
- causes, like God's will, that cannot be hindered produce their effects necessarily;
- what is necessary by its antecedent cause is necessary absolutely, and things God has created relate to the divine will as to an antecedent cause so, if God wills a thing, it comes to pass.

Aquinas' answer is: God's will imposes necessity only on some things willed, which some people explain by secondary causes – that what he produces by necessary causes are necessary, and what he produces by contingent causes contingent. This seems unsatisfactory, because the effect of a first cause may be contingent, due to deficiency in a secondary cause, but this would not stop God's will from producing its effect. Further, if secondary causes are what make the difference between the necessary and the contingent, this would not involve divine intention and will, which cannot be the case. It is better to say that, for the universe's perfection, God wills some things to be done necessarily, others contingently, and so has given some effects necessary causes and others contingent ones. Effects occur contingently, because God wills that they should happen contingently.

His replies to the objections are:

- this must refer to a necessity in the things God wills, which is not absolute, but conditional, for the conditional proposition that, if God wills a thing, it must necessarily be, is necessarily true;
- nothing resists God's will, so the things God wills to happen, happen, and do so necessarily or contingently according to his will;
- the things God brings about have the kind of necessity he wills for them, which may be absolute or conditional, so not everything is necessary absolutely.

Ninth Article   Whether God Wills Evils? (pp. 209–10)

The objections are:

- God seems to will evil, because he wills all good things, and it is good that both evil and good things exist;
- evil adds to the universe's beauty, as it makes the good appear more pleasing and, as God wills everything to do to the universe's perfection and beauty, he wills evil things;

- that evil should exist, and that it should not, are contradictory opposites and, if God wills that evil should not exist, his will is not fulfilled, as evils do exist, so God must will the existence of evil.

Aquinas' answer is: As good and evil are opposed, and we seek good, it is impossible that evil is sought, except accidentally when it accompanies good. The fornicator seeks pleasure, but sin accompanies it. Evil accompanying one good is the privation of another, and would not be sought, even accidentally, if the good to which it is connected were not more desired than the good of which the evil is the privation. God does not will the evil of sin, which is the privation of right order towards the divine good, but he does will the evils of natural defect and punishment, because he wills their accompanying goods. In willing justice, he wills punishment and, in willing the preservation of the natural order, he wills the natural corruption of some things.

His replies to the objections are:

- some have said that, although God does not will evil, he wills that it should be done because, although it is not a good, things evil in themselves are ordered to some good end. However, this is not so, as evil only produces good accidentally – the sinner does not intend that good should flow from his sin, and nothing can be judged by what relates to it accidentally, but only by what belongs to it essentially;
- evil contributes only accidentally to the universe's perfection and beauty, so this conclusion is the result of false premises;
- God does not will evil to be, or not to be, done, but he wills to permit evil to be done, and this is a good.

Tenth Article   Whether God Has Free Choice? (pp. 210–11)

The objections are:

- it seems not, as God alone is not liable to sin, whereas everything else, having free choice, can incline either way;
- free choice is a faculty of reason, by which good and evil are chosen, but God does not will evil, so has no free choice.

Aquinas' answer is: Human beings have free choice in relation to what they do not will of necessity, or by natural instinct; God wills his own goodness necessarily, but not other things, and so he has free choice in relation to them.

The replies to the objections are:

- this does not deny free choice to God absolutely, but in relation to turning to sin;
- as sin involves turning away from the divine goodness, by which God wills all things, it is not possible for him to will sin, but he can choose one of two opposites, and so can will something to be or not.

Question XX   God's Love

First Article   Whether Love Exists in God? (pp. 215–17)

The objections are:

- as love is a passion, and God has no passions, love seems not to exist in God;
- sorrow and anger are not ascribed to God, except by metaphor, so neither is love;
- love is described as a uniting and binding force, but this cannot be the case with God, who is simple.

Aquinas' answer is: There must be love in God, as it is the first movement of the will. Acts of will tend towards good and evil, but good is the will's object essentially, and evil only secondarily. Thus, acts of the will that relate to good are naturally prior to those relating to evil. Further, what is more universal is prior to what is less so. Thus, the intellect is directed first to universal truth, then to particular truths. Now, there are acts of will which regard good under some special condition, as with hope, which regards it as not yet possessed. But love regards good universally, and so is naturally the first act of will – nobody desires or rejoices in anything, except as a good that is loved. So, where there is a will, there must be love, too; and, as God has a will, he must have love.

His replies to the objections are:

- in human beings, the will moves through the medium of the sensitive appetite, which is always accompanied by bodily change, as it affects the heart. Acts of the sensitive appetite, but not acts of will, are called passions. To the extent that it denotes an act of the sensitive appetite, love is a passion, but not to the extent that it is an act of the intellective appetite, and it is in this latter sense that it is in God;

- in passions of the sensitive appetite, there is a material and a formal element, and there is an imperfection in the formal element of many passions (anger, for example, implies sorrow), but not in others, like love. The material element and the imperfection in the formal element in passions cannot be attributed to God, but love (without passion) can be;

- to love someone is to will that person good. Insofar as we love ourselves, we will ourselves good and union with that good, so love is a unitive force, even in God, although there is no composition in him. To love another is to consider the good done to him as done to oneself, and thus it is a binding force, joining another to ourselves, and linking his good to ours. So, too, is the divine love, as God wills good to others, even though there no composition in him.

Second Article   *Whether God Loves All Things?* (pp. 217–18)

The objections are:

- God does not love all things, because love causes the lover to pass into the object of his love, but God does not pass into other things, so it cannot be said that God loves things other than himself;
- God's love is eternal, but other things are only eternal in God, so God only loves things as they exist in him but, if things exist in God, they are not other than himself;
- love is of two kinds, desire and friendship, and God does not have the first kind of love for irrational creatures, because he does not need creatures outside himself, nor can he have friendship with them;
- God hates all doers of wickedness and, as something cannot be loved and hated at the same time, God does not love all things.

Aquinas' answer is: God's will causes all things, so they have being and goodness only in that God wills them. So, God loves everything that exists, because to love a thing is nothing else than to will it good. And, unlike ours, which does not cause the goodness of things, God's love creates goodness in things.

Overview

His replies to the objections are:

- a lover passes into the object of his love, insofar as he wills good to the beloved, and works for his good as for his own;
- creatures have not existed from eternity, except in God but, as they have been in him from eternity, God has known, and loved, them eternally in their proper natures;
- friendship exists only towards rational creatures, capable of returning love, so irrational creatures cannot attain to loving God, whose love for irrational creatures is the love of desire, in that he orders them to rational creatures, and even to himself, not because he needs them, but because of his goodness;
- something can be loved in one respect, and hated in another, so God loves sinners as existing natures, as they are from him, but hates them as sinners.

Third Article   Whether God Loves all Things Equally? (p. 219)

The objections are:

- God seems to love all things equally, as he cares for all equally;
- God's love is his essence, but this does not admit of degree, so he does not love some things more than others;
- God is not said to know or will some things more than others, and this is also the case with his love.

Aquinas' answer is: There are two ways things may be loved: by the act of will, which is more or less intense; and by the good a person wills for the one loved. In the first, God does not love one thing more than another, because he loves all things by one, simple act of the will. However, in the second, he has more love for those things for which he wills a greater good. As God's love causes goodness in things, nothing would be better than anything else if God did not will some things greater good.

His replies to the objections are:

- God cares for all things equally, not by dealing out equal good to all, but by governing all things with equal wisdom and goodness;
- the good God wills for his creatures is not the divine essence, and may vary;
- understanding and willing signify only acts, and do not include in their meaning objects from the diversity of which God may be said to know or will more or less.

Fourth Article   Whether God Always Loves Better Things More? (pp. 220–2)

The objections are:

- God does not love better things more, for Christ was better than the whole human race, but God loved humans more, as he gave Christ up for us all;
- angels are better than human beings, but God loves them more than angels, because it is not angels, but human beings that he helps;
- Peter was better than John, as he loved Christ more, but Christ loved John more than Peter;
- an innocent man is better than a repentant one, but God loves the repentant one more, as he rejoices over him more;
- God loves predestined sinners more than some just men, since he wills them the greater good of eternal life.

Aquinas' answer is: God does love better things more. His will causes goodness in things, and his loving some things more than others is his willing for them a greater good; and this is why some things are better than others.

His replies to the objections are:

- God loves Christ more than the whole created universe, and by his will Christ was true God – Christ's excellence was not lessened when God delivered him up to die to save human beings, for he became thereby a glorious conqueror;

- God loves the human nature, assumed by the Word of God in the person of Christ, more than the angels, and that nature is better, due to union with God. Generally, human and angelic natures are equal in the order of grace although, in the condition of their natures, angels are better than men. God took on human nature, not because he loved humans more, but because of their greater needs;

- Peter's active life shows greater love for God than John's contemplative one, as it indicates greater awareness of life's miseries, and a stronger desire to be free of them, and reach God. However, God loves the contemplative life more, as it does not end with the life of the body. Some say Peter's love for Christ was greater, which was why he was given care of the Church, but that John loved Christ more in himself, and so was entrusted with care of Christ's mother. Other views are that it is uncertain which God loved more; that Peter was loved more for his enthusiasm, and John for his purity; and that Christ loved Peter more for his greater gift of charity, but John more for his intellectual gifts;

- whether innocent or penitent, those who have more grace are better, and better loved and, generally, innocence is more beloved. God is said to rejoice more over the penitent, as he is humble when he rises from sin – also, an equal gift of grace could mean more to the penitent sinner than the innocent;

- God's will causes goodness in things, so the goodness of one that God loves is calculated by the time when some good is given to him. At the time when God gives a greater good to the predestined sinner, he is better than the innocent man, but the opposite is true at other times, and there is a time when he is neither good nor bad.

Question XXI   The Justice and Mercy of God

First Article   Whether there Is Justice in God? (pp. 223–5)

The objections are:

- there seems not to be justice in God, because justice and temperance are members of the same class and, as the latter does not exist in God, the former does not;
- one who does what he wills and pleases does not operate according to justice, so it does not exist in God;
- justice is paying what is due, but God is not in debt to anyone;
- what is in God is in his essence, but justice, unlike good, refers to the act, not the essence.

Aquinas' answer is: There are two kinds of justice: commutative justice, concerned with mutual giving and receiving, which does not relate to God; and distributive justice, as when a ruler justly distributes to his subjects what each deserves. This justice is present in the order of the universe, and shows God's justice.

His replies to the objections are:

- some moral virtues (like temperance) are concerned with passions but, as there are no passions in God, are ascribed him only metaphorically. Other moral virtues, such as justice, relate to giving and concern the will, and these can be ascribed to God;
- God can only will what his wisdom approves, because it is his law of justice, in accordance with which his will is right and just. What he does according to his will, he does justly, as do we, when we act according to law, but our law comes from some higher power, while God is a law unto himself;
- in divine operations, a debt may be due to God or creatures, but God pays what is due – he has a debt to himself that there should be fulfilled in creatures what his will and wisdom contain, which will show his goodness, so here his justice is giving himself his due, and a debt to creatures, that they should have what is due to them and, in this context, he is just when he gives each thing its due, according to its nature and condition, each thing being due what his wisdom orders to it;
- justice relates to acts, but this does not stop it being the essence of God, for something's essence may be a principle of action. Good does not always relate to acts, as something is also good with respect to the perfection in its essence.

Third Article   Whether Mercy Can Be Attributed to God? (pp. 226–7)

The objections are:

- mercy cannot be ascribed to God, as it is a kind of sorrow, of which there is none in God;

- mercy is not becoming to God, as it is relaxation of justice, which God does not do.

Aquinas' answer is: Mercy can be ascribed to God, but in its effect, not as a passion. God does not feel sorrow over human misery, but dispels the defect we call misery. A defect is removed by some kind of perfection of goodness, of which God is the primary source. Giving things perfections also involves God's justice, liberality and mercy. It involves justice, as the perfections are given in accordance with what is due to things. As God gives perfections from goodness, not for his own use, it belongs to liberality; and, as they expel defects, it belongs to mercy.

His replies to the objections are:

- the argument is based on mercy as passion;
- God acts mercifully, not by going against, but by exceeding, his justice, as when a man pardons an offence committed against him, and mercy does not undermine justice, but is its fullness.

Fourth Article   Whether in Every Work of God there Are Mercy and Justice? (pp. 227–8)

The objections are:

- some of God's works are put down to mercy, others to justice;
- Paul said the Jews were converted through justice, the Gentiles through mercy;
- there are many in the world who suffer, which is unjust, and suggests justice and mercy are not found in all God's works;

- as justice concerns paying what is due, and mercy concerns relieving misery, both presuppose something, but creation presupposes nothing, so mercy and justice are not found in it.

Aquinas' answer is: Both are found in all God's works. Mercy is removal of any kind of defect – specifically, those of rational beings, whose lot is to be happy. Whatever God does in created things, he does according to proper order and proportion, which is justice; and this presupposes, and is based on, mercy. Nothing is due to creatures, except on the supposition of something that already exists, or is known in them (for example, a rational soul is due to humans, so that they can be human), and what is due to them depends ultimately on God's goodness. In all his works, there is mercy and, from the abundance of his goodness, he gives creatures what is due to them more generously than they deserve.

His replies to the objections are:

- some of God's works contain more justice than mercy, and vice-versa;
- justice and mercy are present in both conversions, but the justice in the conversion of the Jews is the promises God made to previous generations;
- justice and mercy are present in the punishment of the just, as their lesser faults are cleansed, and they are brought closer to God;
- creation presupposes nothing in the universe, but it does in God's knowledge, and thus justice is preserved in creation: mercy is present in the transition of creatures from non-being to being.

Question XXII   The Providence of God

First Article   Whether Providence Can Suitably Be Attributed to God? (pp. 229–31)

The objections are:

- providence does not belong to God, as it is a part of prudence, which is giving good counsel, and God does not require counsel;
- what is in God is eternal, but providence concerns existing things;
- providence seems composite, as it concerns both intellect and will, but God is not composite.

Aquinas' answer is: Providence must be ascribed to God, as he has created all the good in things, which relates not only to things' substance, but to their being ordered towards an end. As God causes all things, the exemplar of the order of things towards their end necessarily pre-exists in God's mind, which is providence. It is the principal part of prudence, which also comprises recollection of the past and understanding of the present. These enable us to provide for the future. Prudence is directing things towards an end, either for oneself or others, as a ruler does for his subjects. In this second sense, it may be ascribed to God for, in relation to God, nothing can be ordainable towards an end, since he is the last end. In God, providence is the exemplar of the order of things towards an end.

His replies to the objections are:

- taking counsel does not belong to God, but giving commands for the ordering of things towards an end, for the right reason, does, so both prudence and providence belong to God;

- two things relate to providence, the exemplar of order (providence and disposition), which is eternal; and the execution of order (government), which is temporal;
- providence is based in the intellect, but requires the act of willing the end, while prudence, similarly, presupposes the moral virtues, by which the appetitive power is directed towards good. But, it would not affect the divine simplicity, even if providence related to both divine will and intellect, as they are the same thing in God.

Fourth Article   Whether Providence Imposes Any Necessity on what It Foresees? (pp. 236–7)

His replies to the objections are:

- divine providence seems to impose necessity on what it foresees, as effects with essential causes, which they follow necessarily, come to be of necessity, and God's providence is eternal, and precedes its effect, which necessarily flows from it;
- every provider makes his work as stable as possible, to prevent failure and, as God is all-powerful, he gives things the stability of necessity;
- fate, from the immutable source of providence, binds together human acts and fortunes by the indissoluble connection of causes, so providence appears to involve necessity.

Aquinas' answer is: Divine providence imposes necessity on some, but not all, things. Providence concerns ordering things towards an end and, apart from divine goodness, an extrinsic end to all things, their principal good, in themselves, is to perfect the universe, which involves it having all grades of being. Therefore, some things have necessary causes, and other things contingent causes, depending upon their immediate causes.

His replies to the objections are:

- divine providence only requires that things happen somehow, not that they happen only by necessity, so it orders that some things happen by necessity, and others contingently;
- the order of divine providence is unchangeable and certain, and all things happen as foreseen, whether necessarily or contingently;
- this refers to providence's certainty, which always produces its effect, but not always by necessity. Necessity and contingency are consequent upon being, and come under God's foresight, which provides for all being, not just that of causes that provide only for some particular order of things.

Question XXIII   Predestination

First Article   Whether Men Are Predestined by God?
(pp. 238–40)

The objections are:

- we have merit and demerit as masters of our own acts by free choice, so they are not predestined by God;
- all creatures are directed to their ends by divine providence, but other creatures are not said to be predestined, so human beings are not;
- angels, as well as human beings, are capable of beatitude, but predestination does not befit them, as they were never unhappy, so human beings are not predestined;
- the Holy Spirit reveals the benefits God confers upon human

beings to those who are holy, so, if human beings were pre-destined, it would be revealed to all those predestined.

Aquinas' answer is: Everything is subject to God's providence, so he does direct things towards their ends. A rational crea-ture has a twofold end, one of which it can achieve through the power of its nature, but the other is beyond its ability – life eternal. If a thing cannot achieve something through its own power, it needs to be directed towards it, like an arrow by an archer; and God directs rational creatures towards eternal life. The exemplar of that direction pre-exists in God and, when the exemplar of something to be done is in the doer's mind, it is a sort of pre-existence of what is to be done. The exemplar of rational creatures' direction towards eternal life is called predestination, and is part of providence.

His replies to the objections are:

- predestination is imposing necessity after the manner of natural things, which are predetermined towards one end;
- irrational creatures lack the capacity for that end which exceeds the ability of human nature;
- predestination applies to angels, even though they have not been unhappy, for it makes no difference whether or not one is predestined to eternal life from a state of misery;
- even if it were revealed to some, predestination cannot be revealed to all, as it might make those not predestined despair, and those who are, complacent.

Third Article   Whether God Reprobates Any Man?
(pp. 241–3)

The objections are:

- God does not seem to love every man, as he reprobates some, and no one reprobates what he loves;
- if God did, reprobation would have to relate to the reprobate as predestination does to the predestined, but predestination causes the salvation of the predestined, which would make reprobation the cause of the loss of the reprobate, but this cannot be so;
- nothing, which he cannot avoid, should be imposed on anyone but, if God reprobated anyone, he would be bound to perish.

Aquinas' answer is: Predestination is part of providence, involving allowing some defects in things subject to it. God's providence ordains human beings to eternal life, including permitting some to fall away from that end. This is reprobation, which is part of providence in regard to those who turn aside from that end. Just as predestination includes the will to confer grace and glory, reprobation includes the will to permit a person to fall into sin, and to punish them with damnation for it.

His replies to the objections are:

- God loves all men and creatures, but does not wish all of them every good, and is said to reprobate those whom he does not wish to have eternal life;
- predestination causes the glory that is expected in the future life, and the grace received in this life. Reprobation does not cause present sin, but does cause abandonment by God and

eternal punishment, but guilt arises from the free choice of
the person who is reprobated;

• reprobation does not take away from the reprobated person's
power, and it is not absolutely, but only conditionally, impossible for a reprobated person to obtain grace. Although he
cannot acquire grace, his falling into sin comes from his
free desire, so he is rightly held guilty.

Fourth Article   Whether the Predestined Are Elected by God? (pp. 243–4)

The objections are:

• it seems not, for, as the sun shines on all without selection,
so does God's goodness – election is of things that exist, but
predestination from all eternity is also of things that do not,
so some are predestined without election;

• election implies discrimination, but God wills all men to be
saved, so there is no election in predestination.

Aquinas' answer is: Predestination logically presupposes election, which presupposes love. The predestination of some to
eternal salvation logically presupposes that God wills their
salvation, which involves both love (he wishes them this particular good) and election (he wills it for some, in preference
to others, since he reprobates some). Election and love are not
ordered in God in the same way as they are in us. In us, the
will to love does not cause good; rather, we are led to love by an
already existing good. Not so with God, whose will causes that
good that some possess in preference to others. Logically, love
precedes election, which precedes predestination.

His replies to the objections are:

- God communicates his goodness without election, in the sense that all things share in it, but he uses election when communicating particular goods, as he gives certain ones to some, but not others;
- we choose the existing good in things that already exist, but this does not apply to God, who chooses those who do not exist, but he does not err in his choice;
- God wills that all men be saved by his antecedent will, which wills relatively, not absolutely; and not by his consequent will, which wills absolutely.

Glossary

Absolutely perfect. God (Quest. XI, Art. 3) is absolutely perfect (complete, faultless), and so cannot lack any perfection.

Accident. A property of something that is not part of its essence, and which could be added to, or taken away from, it without it ceasing to be the same thing.

Active life. Life dedicated to active service of God, as exemplified by St Peter (Quest. XX, Art. 4).

Actual(ly)/actuality. That which is the case, as opposed to what could become so. Wood is potentially hot, but can only be made hot by something in a state of actuality – fire. God is pure actuality.

Affection of passion. A (strong) feeling. God shows mercy not, as human beings do, because of his feelings, but because of the effects his doing so has: removing human misery (Quest. XXI, Art. 3).

Afflicted persons. People who are suffering.

Agent. One who performs an action.

All grades of being. The universe is better by having different types and grades of being, as it is a place with greater variety, than it would be if it contained beings of only one type or grade (Quest. XXII, Art. 4). The medieval/scholastic view was that things do not just either exist or not exist; there are levels or grades of being, and God is the supreme being and the cause of all other beings.

Ambrose, Saint (c. 339–97). German-born Bishop of Milan and defender of orthodox Roman Catholic teaching.

Ancient philosophers. Philosophers of the ancient world, Greek philosophers.

Angel(s). Heavenly beings who, in the Christian tradition, are well disposed towards human beings and act as God's messengers to them.

Antecedent. Previous, what comes before.

Apprehension. Understanding.

Aristotle (384–322 BC). Greek philosopher and student of Plato. Author of such books as the *De Interpretatione, Nicomachean Ethics* and the *Metaphysics*. His philosophical ideas (Aristotelianism) had an enormous influence on medieval thinkers, such as Thomas Aquinas, who refers to him as 'The Philosopher'.

Artificer. Skilled workman.

Augustine. Saint (354–430). Christian philosopher and theologian, and Bishop of Hippo in North Africa. Author of the *Confessions* and *The City of God*.

Beatified creatures. Those who have been beatified – made happy and blessed.

Beatitude. Perfect happiness/blessedness, which human beings can only achieve after death, when they see God's essence.

Boethius, Anicus Manilus Severinus (c. 480–524). Roman philosopher and consul. Author of the *De Consolatione Philosophae*.

Care of Christ's mother. See John below.

Care of the Church. See Peter below.

Cause/causality. That which brings about a certain effect, as in God being the cause of the universe.

Composite/composition. Something made up of parts – unlike God, in whom there is no composition.

Glossary

Concupiscence. Sexual desire, lust.

Conditional proposition. A proposition the truth of which depends on another proposition, such as, 'If God made the world, we can obtain knowledge about him from the world'.

Consequent(s). That which results, or follows.

Contemplative happiness. The happiness associated with contemplating (looking at, reflecting on, thinking deeply about) something.

Contemplative life. Life dedicated to prayer and reflection, as exemplified by St John (Quest. XX, Art. 4).

Contingent (of existence/effect). That which could not-be, something that might not have occurred and depends on something else for its existence/occurrence. See also necessity below.

Contradictory/contradiction. When a proposition and its negation are brought together.

Corporeal. Bodily.

Created being. Apart from God, who is being itself by his own essence, all being is created being, as it was created by God.

Creature. Something created, including, if God made the world, human beings.

Damnation. The condemnation of the wicked, who are sent to hell.

Defect(s). Fault or shortcoming found in the world, which consists of changeable things.

Defectible. Defective, inadequate.

Deformity of sin. Sin is an offence against, disobedience of, God, which deforms the sinner.

Demon. Evil spirits, who work under the direction of Satan. Jesus is shown casting out, or exorcising, demons in the Gospels.

Determinate effect. Limited, finite effect.

Dionysius, the Areopagite. Paul converted him to Christianity (see Acts 17:34), and he is believed to have been Bishop of Athens. Such books as *On the Heavenly and Ecclesiastical Names*, *On Divine Names* and *On Mystical Theology* are attributed to him, but it is now thought they were written centuries later.

Divine love. God's love. In Christian theology, God is all-loving.

Effect(s). What results from an action. In the *Summa Theologica*, specifically the created world/creatures, which are a source of our knowledge of God, and enable us to establish his existence through the use of natural reason.

Election. Choice, selection.

Esau. Elder son of Isaac, who was tricked out of Isaac's blessing by his younger brother, Jacob. See Genesis 27.

Essence. The essential nature of something, that which makes something what it is, and without which it would not be what it is.

Eternal. In the Christian context, the idea that God transcends time. There is no past, present or future in God, who endures beyond every kind of given duration.

Eternal life. Everlasting life with God after death.

Eternal salvation. Human beings being saved by God, and given eternal life with him.

Evil things. Things opposed to good and to God.

Exemplar. Model or pattern.

Exemplar of that direction pre-exists in God. The pattern of the direction of human beings towards eternal life pre-exists in God. Aquinas explains that, when the pattern of something that is to be done is in the doer's mind, it is a sort of pre-existence of what is to be done. The exemplar of rational creatures' direction towards eternal life is called predestination, which is part of God's providence (Quest. XXIII, Art. 1)

Extrinsic end. External end, end that lies outside something. Aquinas explains that all things in the universe are ordered towards an end. Divine goodness is their extrinsic end (the end that lies outside themselves), but they also have a good or end, in themselves, which is to perfect (complete, make better) the universe (Quest. XXII, Art. 4). See all grades of being above.

False premise(s). A premise is one of the propositions in an argument, on the basis of which the conclusion is reached. If an argument contains a false premise(s), its conclusion will be false.

First agent. God.

First cause. God.

Foreknown. Known beforehand.

Form. Everything that exists has a form, which determines its matter, and thus the kind of thing it is going to be.

Formal element. Aquinas explains (Quest. XX, Art. 1) that passions involve both a formal and a material or physical element. In anger, for example, the formal element is desire for revenge and the material one surging of the blood.

Fornicator. One who has sexual intercourse with somebody to whom he is not married.

Free choice. Choosing freely, being able to choose freely.

Gentiles. Non-Jews.

Genus. Class of things, which have common characteristics, but which can be divided into different species.

Gift of charity. (Active) love of fellow human beings, kindness, willingness to help others.

God. In the *Summa Theologica*, the Christian God.

Grace. The help God freely gives to human beings through Jesus Christ; the means of understanding and accepting in faith what God has revealed of himself to human beings.

His only-begotten son. Jesus Christ. See also Trinity below.

Holy. That which is associated with, devoted to, set apart for, God or religion.

Holy Ghost. See Trinity below.

Holy Spirit. See Trinity below.

Human nature assumed by the Word of God in the person of Christ. Jesus Christ, God's Word, through whom God communicates with human beings, and who became incarnate (took on human nature) to redeem human beings. See also Trinity below.

Immutable. Unchangeable.

Incorporeal. Not bodily, not composed of matter.

Indivisible. That which cannot be divided.

Infinite. Unlimited.

Infinite principle. One that is without limit.

Infuse. Pour or instil something into something else, as God's love does goodness into things (Quest. XX, Art. 2).

Innermostly. To the innermost degree, at the deepest level.

Innocent. One who is not guilty of sin or crime.

Intellect. Mind, faculty of knowing and understanding.

Intellective appetite. Drive, desire associated with the mind, not the senses.

Intelligible form. The idea of something in the mind.

Intermediate causes. Secondary causes that come between God and an effect.

Irrational creatures. Creatures who do not possess reason.

Jacob. Younger son of Isaac. See Esau above and Genesis 27.

Jesus Christ (c. BC 5/6–c. 30 AD). Founder of Christianity, who is the incarnate (took on human nature) Word of God and the second person of the Trinity.

Jerome, Saint (c. 342–420). Italian-born priest and theologian, who first translated the Bible into Latin.

John, Saint (first century). One of Jesus' twelve apostles, to whom tradition attributes the Gospel and Epistles that have his name. Jesus is said to have entrusted the care of his mother to John. See John 19:26, 27.

Just/justice. Treating people fairly, people being treated fairly or receiving their due. In the *Summa Theologica*, there are references both to God's justice and to those who behave justly.

Justification of sinners. Sinners being placed in a right relationship with God, so that they are not damned. How this happens was fiercely disputed by the Roman Catholic Church and the Protestant reformers at the time of the Reformation.

Liberality. Generosity, giving freely.

Life eternal. See eternal life.

Love. Aquinas distinguishes (Quest. XX, Art. 1) between human love which, to the extent that it is an act of the sensitive appetite, is a passion, and God's love, which is an act of the intellective appetite.

Manifold. Many, various.

Martyr(s). Here, one who bears witness to his Christianity by suffering death, rather than give it up.

Material element. See formal element above.

Material things. Things in the material world, physical things.

Matter. That from which physical things are made. The ancient philosophers classified matter into earth, air, fire and water, which were the different forms of primary or prime matter.

Mercy. God's omnipotence is shown especially in his mercy, as he freely forgives the sins of human beings.

Metaphor/metaphorically. Figure of speech that applies names or descriptions to objects in a non-literal way, in order to draw attention to, emphasize, or make clear, some point about them.

Metaphysics/metaphysical. What is after (beyond) physics, and which cannot be investigated by ordinary empirical methods; the investigation of what really exists, of ultimate reality.

Moral virtues. Commendable moral qualities, of which temperance is an example.

More bountifully than is proportionate to their deserts. What is due to his creatures depends entirely on God's goodness, and he gives them what is due to them more generously than they deserve (Quest. XXI, Art. 4).

Natural defect. Defect found in nature. See defect(s) above.

Natural things. Things in nature, the natural world.

Nature. Natural state, condition (Quest. VIII, Art. 1).

Necessary (of existence/effect). That which is not something that could not-be, something that must occur/have occurred.

Necessity of nature. Nothing in nature can cause God to act in a particular way, because God's will is the cause of things, and he acts by his will, not by any necessity of nature (Quest. XIX, Art. 4).

Not determined by any nature (of God). God is supremely being, or being itself; his being is not caused or determined by any nature (Quest. XI, Art. 4).

Ordainable towards an end. God ordains or orders all things towards their end but, as the cause of all things, he is not himself ordainable towards an end, but is the last end of all things (Quest. XXII, Art. 1).

Order of the universe (the). The way God has ordered the universe, which shows forth his justice (Quest. XXI, Art. 1).

Origen (c. 185–c. 254). Christian theologian and teacher, who may have been born in Alexandria. Author of commentaries on the Bible.

Passion. Strong feeling. See also love above.

Paul, Saint (believed to have died 64–68 AD). Christian missionary and theologian who, after his conversion to Christianity, dedicated his life to preaching Christianity to the Gentiles. Paul's letters or epistles to the Christian churches form part of the New Testament.

Perfection. Either perfect quality or being perfected, made perfect.

Per se. As such, in itself.

Peter, Saint (first century). One of Jesus' twelve apostles. Jesus is said to have entrusted the care of the Church to Peter, who became a leader of the Christian community after Jesus' death, and is regarded by the Roman Catholic Church as the first Bishop of Rome. See Matthew 16:18.

Posterior. Later, comes after in a series.

Potential(ly)/potentiality. What could become the case. Wood has the potential to be hot, and becomes actually so when fire (which is in a state of actuality) is applied to it.

Predestined. Determine beforehand. In Christian theology, it is the belief that people's salvation or damnation has been pre-ordained.

Predicate. The part of a statement/proposition in which something is said about the subject. In the statement, 'Socrates is a philosopher', 'is a philosopher' is the predicate.

Pre-exist. Exist before.

Preservation of the natural order. God wills, and thus ensures, that the order of nature is preserved, which involves some things being allowed to undergo natural corruption (Quest. XIX, Art. 9).

Principle of action. The original source of an action.

Privation. A lack or absence of something.

Privative terms. Terms that imply a lack or an absence in something. Our limited understanding of God means that we sometimes use such terms of him (Quest. XI, Art. 3).

Promises made to their fathers. According to Aquinas, God shows justice as well as mercy, when Jews are converted, because of the promises that were made to the Jews, from the time of Abraham, the father of the Jewish nation, which are recorded in the Old Testament (Quest. XXI, Art. 4).

Proposition. Statement, which may or may not be true.

Providence. God's beneficent care and ordering of his creation.

Proximate (of cause/motive-power). Nearest, immediate cause.

Prudence. Carefulness, cautiousness.

Rational creatures. Creatures with reason, human beings.

Rational nature. One with an intellect, reason.

Repentant/penitent. Feeling sorrow or regret (for sin).

Reprobate/reprobation. Cast off, deny salvation to.

Reveals/revelation. What God chooses to disclose of himself to human beings, through, for example, prophets and holy scriptures.

Salvation of the human race. Human beings being saved from sin and death.

Scholastic/scholasticism. The Christian-centred philosophy, taught in medieval universities, of which Aquinas was one of the leading exponents.

Secondary cause. See intermediate cause above.

Seed of Abraham. In Quest. XX, Art. 4, it refers to human beings (as distinct from angels).

Sensitive appetite. Drive, desire associated with the senses, not the mind.

Simplicity/simple (of God). Not consisting of parts, not composite.

Sinners. Those who offend against, disobey, God.

Socrates (c. 470–399 BC). Greek philosopher, who features in the works of Plato, and devoted his life to the pursuit of philosophical truth. He was executed by the Athenian authorities for undermining belief in the gods and corrupting youth.

Some particular order of things. God's providence always produces its effect, but not always by means of necessary causes. The universe contains all grades of being, which makes it a better place. Some of the things in the universe have necessary causes, others contingent ones. Both come under God's foresight, and he does not impose necessity on the latter (Quest. XXII, Art. 4).

Son (the). See Trinity below.

Soul. In Christianity, the spiritual element within human beings, which is the seat of personality and individual identity, which lives on after death, and which will be reunited with its body at the general resurrection.

Substance. The essence of something, which makes it what it is.

Supreme power (of God). God is all-powerful or omnipotent.

Susceptive. Admitting of, receptive to.

Temperance. Moderation, restraint.

Temporal. To do with time and things that are of this world, and therefore subject to the laws of time (and space).

Transition of creatures from non-being to being. God brings things into being in a way that is in keeping with his wisdom and goodness, and he shows his mercy in bringing creatures from non-being into being (Quest. XXI, Art. 4).

Trinity. In Christianity, God exists in three, co-equal persons, Father, Son and Holy Spirit (Ghost) – the Trinity. However, this does not mean that God is divided into three or there are three Gods. God's unity is preserved, because the three persons are of one substance (of one being) and so God is three in one. The teaching has been a subject of debate and (intense) disagreement over the centuries. It is helpful to think in terms of three modes of existence – God the Father: the creator; God the Son: Jesus, the redeemer; and the Holy Spirit: the inspirer and sustainer of Christians and the Christian Church.

Tyrant(s). An absolute, and usually oppressive, ruler.

Union with the Godhead. Being united with God. See Trinity above.

Unitive force. Force that unites.

Unity (of God). Oneness. God is perfect oneness, one reality.

Unity of the world. The world, under God's direction, shows unity, as the things in it are ordered to each other, as some serve others (Quest. XI, Art. 3).

Virtue(s). See moral virtues above.

Vision of God. When human beings will see God's essence. See also beatitude above.

Voluntary agent(s). Agent who acts as a result of reason and choice.

Will. Generally, the capability of wishing for something and using one's mental powers to try to accomplish it. Aquinas discusses God's will in Question XIX.

Workers of iniquity. Those who do wicked or unjust things.

The Briefly Series

Briefly: Anselm's *Proslogion*
Briefly: Aquinas' *Summa Theologica I*
Briefly: Aquinas' *Summa Theologica II*
Briefly: Descartes' *Meditations on First Philosophy*
Briefly: Hume's *Dialogues Concerning Natural Religion*
Briefly: Kant's *Groundwork of the Metaphysics of Morals*
Briefly: Mill's *Utilitarianism*
Briefly: Mill's *On Liberty*
Briefly: Plato's *The Republic*